I HEARD THEIR CRY

The Forgotten Souls

SHIRLEY BOWERS

Dedication

To the thousands of men, women and children who during the 17th Century were taken from the British Isles and transported to Barbados against their will.

I HEARD THEIR CRY

Copyright © 2025 Shirley Bowers

Paperback ISBN: 978-1-915223-45-6

All rights reserved.

No part of this publication may be reproduced, stored in a retrieval system, or transmitted in any form or by any means, electronic, mechanical, photocopying or otherwise, without prior written consent of the publisher except as provided under United Kingdom copyright law. Short extracts may be used for review purposes with credits given.

Unless otherwise indicated, all Scripture quotations are from The Passion Translation®. Copyright © 2017, 2018, 2020 by Passion & Fire Ministries, Inc. Used by permission. All rights reserved. ThePassionTranslation.com.

Scripture quotations marked NIV are taken from THE HOLY BIBLE, NEW INTERNATIONAL VERSION®, NIV® Copyright © 1973, 1978, 1984, 2011 by Biblica, Inc.® Used by permission. All rights reserved worldwide.

Scripture quotations marked MSG are taken from *THE MESSAGE*, copyright © 1993, 2002, 2018 by Eugene H. Peterson. Used by permission of NavPress. All rights reserved. Represented by Tyndale House Publishers, Inc.

Published by

Maurice Wylie Media

Your Inspirational & Christian Book Publisher

For more information visit
www.MauriceWylieMedia.com

Acknowledgements

I would like to begin by acknowledging Vanessa Murphy. She is not only a dear friend and team member, but also my editor. Thank you so much for the hours of hard work and dedication you have put into this book. There are not enough words to express how much you are appreciated. Another dear friend is Annette Quail who has been a valued team member since 1998. Thank you both for your unwavering support and for sharing this amazing journey with me.

For everyone who has previously travelled with me and played an active role in Arise Ministries, including our current prayer council, as well as the many prayer partners around the globe. This is true unity and we are grateful to you all.

I want to remember also those who were part of this story, but have now passed away; My husband Tony of 51 years, who made a point of praying us off on many of our trips. Fred Watson, who was the oldest direct descendant in Barbados and the recipient of the letter of apology, and other dear friends whose absence is felt so very deeply.

Finally, a huge thank you to my family for their love and support. A special mention to my son Jonathan for all his technical help and the amazing video he produced explaining our Barbados Project.

I really could not have done this without you all.

Foreword

*'He raises the poor from the dust
and lifts the needy from the ash heap;
he seats them with princes,
with the princes of their people.'*

Psalm 113:7-8.

You have in your hands a story that is, in every sense, remarkable.

First and foremost, *I heard Their Cry* tells the story of our remarkable God - of the Great *I AM*: Of the God who is love - and who shows us the fullness of that love in and through His Son, Jesus Christ; Of the God who is faithful and just; And of the God who never forgets His own, especially the marginalised, the exploited, abused, betrayed and voiceless ones. As the author of Psalm 113 reminds us, such people are not forgotten and will one day be 'lifted up' and 'seated with princes'.

Next, this book speaks powerfully and with passion into a world that needs so desperately to know the remarkable power that is to be found in what St Paul describes as, 'the ministry of reconciliation.'[1] *I Heard Their Cry* reminds us that reconciliation is at the very heart of the Gospel. It isn't an optional extra. As those who have been caught-up in, and captivated and transformed by, the life and story of the God who is 'reconciling the world to Himself in Christ', so we are called to be agents of that reconciliation amid so much pain, distortion and brokenness. If that feels frightening, read on and be inspired and encouraged! As well as telling a particular story, I suggest that this book also offers what I've come to think of as a 'framework of faith' about how we might bring the reconciling light and love of Jesus Christ to the people, places and situations where God has called us.

---
[1] 2 Corinthians 5:19.

Finally, although she would never say so because of her humility, *I Heard Their Cry* reminds us of the difference that one remarkable, prayerful, faithful, obedient and loving human being can make. I honestly believe this book has the potential to change lives, communities and, yes, even nations. Shirley heard God's call and, despite the self-doubt that she, like so many before her, experienced, believed in Him sufficiently to say, "Here I am. Send me!" Shirley, along with Annette, Vanessa and all those in Arise and beyond who support her, are embodying, living and sharing with others, the ministry of reconciliation. More than that, they're encouraging us to do the same.

To that all-important question that God asked Isaiah, *"Whom shall I send? And who will go for us?",* how will you reply?

Soli Deo Gloria!

Reverend Scott Watts
Huntingdon
July 2024

Contents

Acknowledgements		7
Foreword		9
Introduction		13
1.	Echoes of Forgotten Voices	15
2.	From Green Fields to Sugar Fields	19
3.	Paths to Healing and Reconciliation	27
4.	Tracing the Steps of the Displaced	33
5.	I Am Who I Am	39
6.	Divine Encounters	49
7.	The Stage is Set	55
8.	Planting Hope in a Broken World	65
9.	River of Life	73
10.	A Connecting Bridge	77
11.	Unearthing History	91
12.	Every Life Matters	95
13.	A Ball of Daisies	103
14.	Birds of Paradise	109
15.	Love Never Dies	117
16.	Honouring the Past	121
17.	The Descendants	129
18.	Coming Home	137
19.	Stepping into another World	143
20.	Island of Secrets and Surprises	147
21.	New Roots	157
22.	Full Circle	163
23.	Celebrations of Remembrance	171
Contact		183

Introduction

The nations of the British Isles have a complex and contentious past. Even a fleeting look through the history books leaves us in no doubt that the actions of past leaders have had far-reaching consequences - consequences that have often been felt globally. However, we cannot ignore the impact of historical wrongs. Although most keenly felt by those on the receiving end at the time, they still have a ripple effect through the centuries. In cases where wrongs have been left unchallenged by subsequent generations, it leaves the descendants of those who were wronged still suffering. This can shape the futures of entire people groups.

One man who is likely to remain a figure of controversy is English Civil War leader Oliver Cromwell. I live in the market town of Huntingdon in the Huntingdonshire district of Cambridgeshire, England, his birthplace, and for over 25 years I have been seeking to bring healing and reconciliation to the Cromwell part of history. This journey has taken me to many places, including Ireland and Scotland, and now Barbados.

Barbados is undoubtedly a beautiful island and a tourist destination for thousands. You only need to travel down the west coast to see it is a hot spot for the rich and famous. However, travel the 14 miles to the east coast and it's an entirely different story. Here, over centuries, some of the White population have lived in isolation and poverty. There is much ignorance and misunderstanding of their situation. During the Civil War in the 17th Century, Cromwell and his parliament transported Prisoners of War, Royalist soldiers and Catholic landowners to Barbados, as well as other places. This has been debated over the years, but extensive research proves this truth can no longer be denied. Descendants of these transportees in Barbados still live with the weight of this history. Thankfully things have improved in recent years, but there are many who still feel stigmatised. These people and their descendants are part of the history of Ireland and the British Isles, as well as Barbados, and they deserve to be recognised and respected as such.

This book tells not only my story but their story too.

CHAPTER 1

Echoes of Forgotten Voices

As I sit ready to write this story and ponder where to begin, I feel overwhelmed. All I can see in my head is a picture of a young man who lived well over 350 years ago, in the 17th Century. A young man who left home one day to help defend his country, only he never returns. He never gets married or has a family and he will never see his homeland again. His story is largely unknown, yet it is tied up with mine. How can that be? We're not related or even from the same country. Yet his eyes speak volumes as they seemed to be saying "Thank you for telling my story."

What is his story?

Let me take you on a journey; a journey that spans many years, a journey of discovery as well as pain. It is a journey that tells not only his story, but the story of thousands whose faces we will never see, who for many years were forgotten and hidden in the shadows. Come and share not only my story, but their story too and how they finished up on the faraway island of Barbados.

How I came to be doing this is told in my first book, *From History to Hope,* and a short summary may help you understand my approach. It began back in the 1980s when a new minister came to my Methodist church in the small town of Huntingdon, England. I was struggling with issues connected to my anxiety and low self-esteem. Through his ministry, I began to uncover some deep wounds in my life. I came to realise how the negative words spoken over me had affected the way I thought about myself and, in turn, how I reacted to others. Little by little, through the care and support of many people, I was encouraged to forgive and let go of my pain. It wasn't always easy, but it was through this process that I began to understand how God's love brought healing to my own personal history.

As time went on, I came to realise that just as my past had affected me, the same could be true for a family, a church, a town, a village and even a nation. Every unjust act has consequences. With this insight, I began to look at my hometown of Huntingdon. It has previously been described in the media as one of the unhappiest places to live in England. I wondered why people are so unhappy in this town and began to research the history of Huntingdon in an attempt to answer these questions. I knew it was the birthplace of the English Civil War leader Oliver Cromwell, but that was all I knew. I set myself the task of finding out about this man, known as 'Huntingdon's most famous son'. I discovered he was a Puritan with strong religious views and was particularly against any form of idolatry. I was shocked to learn of the role he played in beheading King Charles I in 1649 and the subsequent invasion of Ireland. It was obvious that his attitude towards Catholics, especially Irish Catholics, had led to much bloodshed and deep division in the land. Most significant to me was that Cromwell states in his campaign letters that he did it in the name of God or Christ, and led by the Holy Ghost. This greatly disturbed me. I wanted to do something about it but didn't know what.

It was at this point in the late 1990s, that others felt the call to join me. Annette Quail was the first, and then Vanessa Murphy in 2000. As we met and prayed together, it became very clear that we shared a deep desire for healing and reconciliation. From this, Arise Ministries was born and these ladies became committed team members. Others joined us for a season; Rosemary, Isla and Val to name but a few, and many have joined us as prayer partners, both locally and across the globe.

Over the years as we travelled to Ireland, we came across people who literally cursed Huntingdon for giving birth to Oliver Cromwell. One particular time will always stand out. I was taking part in a prayer walk around Ireland. One evening, a gentleman came to ask me, what I knew and felt about Cromwell. I panicked as I didn't know where to start. So, I simply told him that when I discovered what happened during Cromwell's time in Ireland, it made me feel ashamed that he came from my town. I continued, "I long to do something to try and address this shameful part of our history and hopefully bring some healing, but I don't know what." He went quiet for a while, then he told me that he had prayed for a long time for God to send someone to deal with this issue. I could see the pain went very deep. He continued, "Shirley, I have a confession to make. I live in the north of England, but I actually come from Dublin. My work takes me up and down the A1 Road a lot and every time I pass Huntingdon, I speak out, 'No good thing will ever come out of that town. It's a place of death. Now here I am, sitting with someone from there who has a heart to see healing in my land. How dare I say such a thing. I am so, so sorry."

It was clear to me from then on, that the unjust actions of Oliver Cromwell had left a painful and bitter legacy that still affects people today. I knew we had to do something to help bring healing, both for the Irish people and for Huntingdon. We are not 'pro' or 'anti' Cromwell and it has never been about judging him. However, it is important to address the consequences of his actions. As I live in Cromwell's birthplace I felt I owed it to the Irish people to revisit those places he had been and somehow express how sorry I was for what happened and the pain it had left behind.

We began to share our thoughts with civic and church leaders in Huntingdon. Some were very enthusiastic while others were unsure, but as they listened to our thoughts, they agreed to support our plans. Next, we had to be sure that people in Ireland agreed too. Cromwell had already invaded Ireland, so it was important to us not to do the same. This meant getting permission from civic and church leaders.

So, in spring 2002, along with Phyllis Forsythe from Northern Ireland, followed Cromwell's route around the Republic of Ireland. We met with leaders and church members, sharing our hope to help bring healing to this deep wound. Our plans were well received in every place we visited and we were invited to return later that year.

As Drogheda was the first town Cromwell took over on September 11, 1649, it was an appropriate time and place for us to begin our journey. We carried with us a letter of apology from Huntingdon Churches Together which read;

> *Dear Friends*
>
> *We the members of Churches Together in Huntingdon warmly greet our brothers and sisters in the churches and towns of Drogheda, Wexford and elsewhere in Ireland.*
>
> *We want you to know that in our hearts we fully support the reconciliation, Christian love and fellowship that this walk represents. Our town has for many years been associated with Oliver Cromwell. In the local churches we recognise the pain his coming to Ireland meant and still means. For this we are deeply sorry.*
>
> *Our hope is that through this walk we will share time together, which will show the unity for which our Saviour prayed.*
>
> *May the Lord bless you and bring you peace. May your lovely land know His abundant blessing.*
>
> *As Christian friends we send our greetings in the name of our Saviour and Lord Jesus Christ.*

Our actions, together with this letter, touched many lives and started a healing process that is still ongoing.

It turned out to be just the beginning for us all.

CHAPTER 2

From Green Fields to Sugar Fields

It was during that trip in 2002, that I met a lady in Wexford who gave me a book she had just read, *To Hell or Barbados* by Sean O'Callaghan.[2] She believed I should read it too. The book is an in-depth account of the transportation of Irish men, women and children to Barbados and North America in the 1650s. In the introduction of his book, Sean explains how he wanted to find out what happened to them, as there is no record of any having ever returned. He went to great lengths to uncover the truth. He writes,

> *"Although I am not an historian, I determined to find out. There are no Irish records. They were destroyed when the Public Records Office in Dublin was burned in 1922. The State Papers in the English Public Records Office in Kew yielded some information, as did the Shipping Register of the period, giving details of some of the ships engaged in the transportation as well as the names of their masters, but this was not enough..."*

He felt the answer must be in Barbados, so he wrote to the Barbados Museum and Historical Society. Three weeks later, he received a letter informing him that the library contained a quantity of files regarding Irish, Scottish and African slaves. This, Sean said, was more than he

---
[2] Sean O'Callaghan was born in Killavullen, Co Cork in 1918. He was commissioned in the Irish Army in 1936. On leaving the army he became a journalist in Fleet St, as well as in Nairobi. He published his first book, The Easter Lily, in 1956, and became a full-time writer. He died as To Hell or Barbados went to press, in August 2000.

could have hoped for, and he left for Barbados in 1993, where he spent the next four years researching for himself the full extent of what happened to the deportees. I had known about the deportation of the Irish to the West Indies and North Virginia by Cromwell and his Parliament, but had never studied it in detail. Being dyslexic, it took me quite a while to get my head around the historical details and evidence in Sean's book. However, in 2007, with the manuscript of my first book at the publishers, I decided it was a good time to start reading it. As it turned out, it was the perfect time - that year was the 200th Anniversary of the Abolition of the Slave Trade.

I did not find it an easy read, but the more I read, the more it broke my heart. I was shocked at how the people had been treated. Sean describes how Cromwell used the slave trade as a way to clear the land of Prisoners of War, Royalists and Catholics, and, in the process, to populate the Commonwealth. Some went as indentured labourers; others were sold to slave ships. If they became too sick on the journey they would be thrown overboard, as more money could be claimed on insurance than if they were sold in this condition. On landing, they were all treated appallingly, with no respect. As I read the details, which I will not repeat, I felt sick. How could anyone treat fellow humans in this inhumane way?

Sean discovered that there is still a group of direct descendants of those transported. They live in isolation on the east of the island and are known as 'Poor Whites' or 'Red Legs'. It is believed the name 'Red Legs' was first applied to the Irish and Scots when they reached Barbados and because they were wearing kilts, their legs were soon burnt in the sun. Sadly, as we discovered later, this derogatory term endures and is offensive to those on the receiving end. Some descendants have managed to build a new life, but for too many it continues to be a stigma. They feel discriminated against, especially when looking for work, which keeps them in poverty. The day before he was leaving Barbados, Sean made one last effort to make contact with these people, but he was driven off their land. He wrote,

> *"It was a melancholy outing and although I was glad to be back in the gaiety and bustle of the hotel, I could not get the Red Legs out of my mind. Perhaps somebody somewhere will do something to ease their plight."*

This hit me hard. I wept. I knew I had to do something.

Sean continued,

> *"It is my fervent hope that Catholic families in Ireland who, according to Reverend Aubrey Gwynn,[3] 'count it among the proudest memories of their history that some representatives of their name were thus sold in the West Indies,' will band together and do something for their long-forgotten brethren - the Red Legs of Barbados."*

Sadly, Sean died before the book was published in the year 2000, but I hope he knows the cry of his heart has been heard.

I resolved to reread his book but found it was no easier to read a second time. However, I felt I owed it to the people to try in some small way to understand what they had been through. I was heartbroken that someone from my town could be responsible. I tried to reason it out by thinking maybe Cromwell did not know what sort of life he was sending them to. I even questioned whether it really happened. Many people would justify his action by saying 'That was what they did in those days'. However, I knew in my heart this was wrong and nothing, absolutely nothing, can make it right. To take people from their land, almost certainly against their will, and ship them off to a foreign country, knowing they would never return, nor see their family again - this was not only cruel and unjust but inhumane. Why had we not heard this tragic story before? The more I thought about it, the more I could see that we, as humans, may have forgotten those people, but God never had. I knew beyond doubt I was being prompted to do something, even though I had no idea what. I shared

---
[3] An historian.

my thoughts with Annette and Vanessa and over the next few days, no matter where we turned, everything kept pointing towards slavery. We felt sure we were being encouraged to dig deeper.

We began by researching for ourselves Cromwell's letters that Sean quoted, to see if what he had written was the truth. Vanessa and I visited the archives in the Houses of Parliament in London and Cambridge University Library where his campaign letters are stored. As you can imagine, these documents are difficult to read, but they undeniably prove that this really did happen. It is true—we saw the evidence for ourselves.

For example;

On arrival back in Dublin in September 1649, Cromwell sent letters to the Government in London describing the storming of Tredah (now Drogheda);

> *It hath pleased God to bless our endeavours at Tredah. After battery, we stormed it. The enemy were about 3,000 strong in the Town... I believe we put to the sword the whole number of defendants. I do not think Thirty of the whole number escaped with their lives. Those that did, are in safe custody for the Barbadoes."*[4].......

In another letter the following day, he graphically described how these soldiers were dealt with,

> *"When they submitted, their officers were knocked on the head; and every tenth man of the soldiers killed; and the rest shipped for the Barbadoes. The soldiers in the other tower were all spared, as to their lives only; and shipped likewise for the Barbadoes."*[5]....

---

[4] Oliver Cromwell's Letters and Speeches, Thomas Carlyle; Part V, Letter CIV, Page 49.
[5] As above, Letter CV, see page 89.

Later there were letters from Henry Cromwell, Oliver's son, to the Council of State, about the deportation of young girls and boys to the West Indies, particularly Jamaica, to help populate the Commonwealth, in 1655;

> *"Concerninge the younge women, although we must use force in takeinge them up, yet it beinge so much for their owne goode, and likely to be soe great advantage to the publique, it is not in the least doubted, that you may have such a number of them as you shall thinke fitt to make use uppon this account."*[6]

Over the next weeks, Henry Cromwell continued to request authority from the Council of State to carry out the task. In a letter Sean quoted from October 1655, Secretary Thurloe wrote to H Cromwell, Major General of the Forces in Ireland;

My Lord

I did hope to have given your lordship an account by this post of the buissines of causing younge wenches and youths in Ireland to be sent into the West-Indies; but I could not make things readye. The committee of the council have voted 1,000 girls, and as many youths be taken up for that purpose.... Council of State under Cromwell orders that one thousand Irish girls, and the like number of youths of 14 years or under be sent to Jamaica."

If you are interested in researching this further for yourself, Sean O'Callaghan's book, *To Hell or Barbados*,[7] is a good starting point. Records can also be found at *British History Online*.

Cromwell believed he was doing this all in the name of God, but that is not the God I believe in. Tears flowed and my heart cried out; What can I do? Where do I start?

---

[6] A Collection of the State Papers of John Thurloe, Volume 4, Sept 1655 - May 1656. (September 11, 1655)
[7] To Hell or Barbados, published by Brandon, 2001.

As we prayed about it, we felt certain we should share this revelation with others, especially those in Ireland. We decided that when my book was available, we would go on a book tour and at the same time, talk about Sean's findings and see if people had heard the story.

With this in mind, we concentrated our prayers on the publication of the book as everything rested on its release. One evening, our friend Rosemary had a picture of a ruby gemstone. The following year was my Ruby (40th) wedding anniversary and we knew that in the Bible, 40 is a significant number. For example, Moses and the Israelites spent 40 years in the desert; Jesus, before His ministry began, spent 40 days in the wilderness. What could this mean for us? Rosemary suddenly started to laugh, remarking how slow we had been to remember there are 40 weeks of pregnancy. We had said previously that getting the book published was like giving birth. So, we counted 40 weeks since the publisher, Gottfried Bernard, had picked up the manuscript and we marked the date on the calendar. A day or so later, I had a phone call from Gottfried saying that the book would go to print on the very day we had marked.

A week or so later, a friend asked to speak to me after church. He is from Northern Ireland and his mother-in-law was visiting from its capital Belfast. A friend of hers had sent their church's newsletter and she showed him what she was reading,

> *"In the 1650s, Cromwell sent thousands, perhaps as many as 50,000, Irish men and women to Barbados, Montserrat, St Kitts and Antigua. The question remains, how was it that even those who had a deep Christian faith could be so blind to the evil of slavery?"*

She asked him, "Hasn't someone from your church written about Cromwell?" I could hardly believe my ears. I now felt even stronger that we needed to return to Ireland and share about this injustice.

It was in June 2007, Annette, Vanessa and I set off for Dublin. We were excited but also apprehensive. We had no idea how Sean's book would be received, let alone mine. However, reassurance came when we arrived at the ferry port and on-boarding, were directed to park on the 'Ruby' deck. As we have said many times, you could not make this up!

Situated on the east coast of Ireland, Drogheda is 75 miles south of Belfast and 34 miles north of Dublin. It was the first of many receptions. The Deputy Mayor remarked in his welcome address that, "You have three former mayors here today, which shows how much respect Arise Ministries has here in Drogheda." He went on to say that he believed that what we had done in 2002, by expressing regret for Cromwell's actions, had brought a change in the atmosphere and new life to the town. "My deep desire is for this healing and reconciliation to continue across the community" he said in closing. Tom Reilly, a local historian and author, who once opposed what we were doing, spoke next. He shared how, even though he does not believe in God himself, because Cromwell did what he did 'in the name of God,' he could appreciate why we, as Christians, were doing this. He went on to show great respect for me by saying, "Well done, Shirley," he said more than once, "it's no mean task producing a book." This was a real turn around! I was asked to respond and took the opportunity to tell them what I had learned about the 'Poor Whites'. It had a profound effect on those there that morning. So many people were astonished that they did not know anything about this. It was as if these people have truly been erased from the pages of history.

We continued our journey to Dublin and then on south for nearly 100 miles to Wexford. Over breakfast one morning, our host, Stephen, received a phone call from Father Jim Finn, who we had met in 2002. He had prayed specifically about the Cromwell issue for eight years before we met. I do not know why, but I remember saying, "I have a feeling this man will be coming with us to Barbados." Seconds later, we heard Stephen's excited voice saying, "*You are looking into Barbados too!*" Jim explained that after our last visit, he had read Sean's book and been challenged by this dreadful story. He had a deep desire to go to Barbados and had been praying since then for revelation on when that should be. We were very excited by this and made arrangements to meet up at a former harbour where the slave ships had picked up their human cargo. A small group had gathered by the time we arrived. They shared with us the recent tragedy of a young woman who took her life and those of her two children. *"No-one heard her cry for help,"* they said. This seemed to be mirroring the unheeded cries of those who had been put on those slave ships years earlier. It was a very emotional prayer time as we remembered that young mum and her torment, as well as those people centuries ago.

Nearing the end of our trip, we drove 120 miles northwest up to Athlone, where I had been invited to speak at a local prayer gathering. There was a real sense of expectation as we worshipped together and I felt privileged to share the story you have just read. As I was speaking, I became aware of a gentleman close to me who was becoming more and more distressed. As my talk came to its conclusion, he asked if he could speak. He introduced himself as David Shirley and explained how affected he had been when he had met me back in 2002, when we shared in an act of reconciliation between Catholics and Protestants on Athlone Bridge. He said he did not understand then why it had touched him as deeply as it did, so he spoke to his family. They informed him that an ancestor of theirs came from the English family of 'Shirley,' who had come over to Ireland with Oliver Cromwell. So, as I was sharing that night, he realised his ancestor could easily have been involved in this awful trade in human lives. He started to weep, saying over and over, "I am so sorry, I am so sorry." My heart went out to him and I knew that this man would also be coming with us to Barbados.

Every day the encouragement grew as we travelled from place to place. My book was going down well, but more importantly, people were catching the vision and promising to pray for their 'forgotten brethren in Barbados.'

CHAPTER 3

Paths to Healing and Reconciliation

We now had a better understanding of the need to seek forgiveness for this dreadful act. However, as we still had no idea where to begin, we set time aside to pray and seek direction. During those months, our daily Bible reading notes were based on the book of Nehemiah. As Nehemiah had helped to direct us ahead of our 2002 trip, I was curious to see if anything would be highlighted this time.

Nehemiah, a Jewish leader, was in exile when he heard that the wall of Jerusalem was broken down. He knew that this sacred city and its temple were now vulnerable to attack from their enemies. He wept for days and while he was praying about it, he felt a burden to return to rebuild the wall. However, first, he needed permission from the Persian king he served, and that was not going to be easy.

So, what were the lessons we needed to learn this time?

> Nehemiah did not need to say anything, as it was the king who noticed something was wrong. So, **be patient**.

1) **Timing is particularly important.** The right action can turn out to be the wrong one simply because it was the wrong time. We needed to stay alert for signs to determine the what, how and when.

2) Nehemiah sends up a quick prayer before he answers the king. **Prayer is key.**
   We needed to pray for those people in authority, both here and in Barbados, to recognise the need to bring justice to the Poor Whites.

3) It is important we do our **research** and find out what is known about these forgotten people.

Even after Nehemiah received permission from the king to return to Jerusalem, his enemies tried to prevent him from completing the task of rebuilding the wall. We could see that there was a battle ahead of us too. Like Nehemiah's, our task looked too big, too difficult and we could so easily become overwhelmed. However, a quote from Corrie Ten Boom[8] came to mind,

> *"Faith sees the invisible, believes the incredible and receives the impossible."*

After Nehemiah, the next book in the Bible is Esther, which tells the story of how, even under the threat of her life, Queen Esther went before the king to plead for her people, the Jews. Haman, a high-ranking royal official, was secretly plotting to annihilate the entire Jewish population. She had been told that they would be destroyed if she kept silent. I could see that, in the same way, Cromwell and his Parliament tried to get rid of Irish Catholics and Royalists in the most inhumane way. Even though it was over 350 years ago, it still affects people today, as the Poor Whites in Barbados know only too well. So I, like Queen Esther and Nehemiah, cannot stay silent. I too need to speak to people in authority, both here and in Barbados. But how?

---

[8] Corrie ten Boom, a Dutch Christian watchmaker and Holocaust survivor. She is known for her inspirational writings and speeches on faith, forgiveness, and resilience.

During this same time in 2007, I heard from Gottfried that the German translation of *From History to Hope* was to be launched at a conference in Switzerland that September, so Rosemary and I arranged to go. I knew this was important to Gottfried, but little did I realise how significant it was going to be for my healing too. I had never been to Switzerland before and was in awe of the magnificent snow-capped mountains. The following morning, we met the leader of the conference. He was so enthusiastic about the book and couldn't wait to encourage me. "It is my belief, that the work you have done in Ireland will open the way for Queen Elizabeth II to visit the Irish Republic one day," he said. I wasn't sure about that; however, it proved to be a prophetic word. She made that historic visit four years later in 2011.

The book launch went well and I felt good sharing a small part of its story. However, my confidence dropped when I learned we were to go and pray at the top of the Niesen Mountain. It made me extremely anxious because I had nothing appropriate to wear. What on earth was I going to do? I shared this with my host and she offered me a pair of her husband's boots (Did I tell you I have big feet!). This was helpful, but I still needed trousers. So, the following day, I had to run into town to find something suitable to wear. I was panicking the whole time.

As the cable car ascended through the clouds, it stirred something deep in me, but at this point I did not have a clue why. Once we arrived at the viewing platform, the clouds separated and the sun came out. What a breathtaking view! We were all encouraged to pick up a stone to represent something that we would like to remove from our lives and throw it over the side, then pick up another stone to replace it with the right thing. For example, forgiveness in place of unforgiveness, love replacing hate, and so on. All I could think about was my panic over clothes, so my first stone represented this, which I replaced with peace.

Later, when I was alone, I prayed. I needed to understand why this had affected me so deeply. I started to realise how many times I had worn the wrong clothes. This conference, for instance, was held in a sports hall and everyone was dressed in very casual clothes, ski jackets and the like, but I was in summer dress. I began to remember more occasions. Being the third child, my parents could not afford to buy my school uniform like they had for my brother and sister. When my brother got married, Mum would not buy me the same bridesmaid dress as the others. I began to cry as more memories flooded my mind. I remembered my fear and panic going to school, knowing I would get into trouble because I was not dressed correctly. This pattern continued throughout my life and I recalled the anxiety and panic I always felt when deciding what to wear. I knew I needed to voice my forgiveness towards my mum and dad. This I did willingly, for I knew they had done their best. After a while, as I remembered what happened on the mountain, I was filled with a deep peace. Tears flowed again, but this time they were healing tears.

Back home, I turned my attention to Barbados, and over the next few weeks, I spent many days and even nights praying for these forgotten people. I remember sometimes just weeping as I recalled how they were made to feel so worthless. How can I possibly do anything that would put this right?

Towards the end of the year, to my surprise, Father Jim Finn in County Wexford, messaged he was coming to visit Huntingdon. I hadn't heard any more from him since the book tour when he shared his heart for the people in Barbados, so I was curious to see what his visit was about. He told us he wanted to meet church leaders in our town, and Vanessa and I were astonished as we listened to him share how we met back in 2002 and why coming to Huntingdon was important to him. The reason, he said, was to share the healing God had done for him. "Shortly after Shirley's visit," he told them, "I woke one day and saw England as if for the first time. The veil had been lifted. Now I have a love for England that I have never had before." I was taken aback as he had never mentioned this to us. It just shows how deep this wound is and how love in action can bring healing.

Early in January 2008, Father Finn got in touch again, to tell me that he had been in contact with Father Harcourt, the priest at St Patrick's Catholic Cathedral in Bridgetown, Barbados and was planning a visit later that month. I was pleased for him, but I knew it was not the right time for me to go as Tony, my husband, was seriously ill in hospital. The days were long as I sat by his bedside and my thoughts often turned to Father Finn and how he was getting on. Even though I believed I had been called to go myself, how on earth was I going to answer that call? Thousands of people all over the world suffer the consequences of deep-rooted generational wounds. I cannot help everyone, but I desperately wanted to do something for this group in Barbados. As I was thinking about this, a picture came into my head of me weeping as I knelt before the Poor Whites, expressing remorse and asking for their forgiveness.

By the end of February, Tony had made a good recovery. Father Finn returned with news that we would be welcome in Barbados anytime, but we were still no wiser as to when this might be. So, I reread *To Hell or Barbados* and what caught my attention this time was how Cromwell's Parliament quickly passed laws to enable them to clear the land of Ireland of 'undesirables' (their words) by deporting them. For example, the Act for the Settling of Ireland, or Act of Settlement as it is better known, was passed in 1652. It enabled them to confiscate land and either execute or deport those found guilty of participating in the Rebellion of 1641, as well as Irish Catholics who had taken no part but had 'remained quiet', or any Irish Catholics or Anglo-Irish who had fought against Cromwell. All deportations had to be completed by May 1, 1654. With this knowledge, I felt sure we needed to go to Barbados ourselves before May to see if all we had read was true.

CHAPTER 4

Tracing the Steps of the Displaced

As we prepared for this fact-finding trip, prayer remained our priority. We felt drawn towards Psalm 126 which speaks of captives returning home. We read, *"Those who sow with tears, will reap with songs of joy."* We believed this was a promise for the descendants of those who had been torn from their land and loved ones.

Although this trip was not a holiday, we were extremely excited as we set off that April morning in 2008 and as we arrived at Gatwick Airport, I said to Annette and Vanessa, "I wonder what we will see this time to show us we are on track." As we made our way towards the plane, I looked across the tarmac and could hardly believe my eyes; on the side of our plane was the name *Ruby Tuesday*. Furthermore, we asked the flight attendant if it was possible to move to seats with more leg room and were moved to row 40. As rubies and the number 40 had played a prominent part in our story before, we were encouraged. Our next adventure had begun!

We stayed with Jean, one of Father Harcourt's parishioners. We knew we were in the right place when she told us how her ancestor was deported from England. When Father Harcourt arrived, he too told us that even though he was not White, he was descended from an Irish slave. "Most people here are and they have Irish surnames," he said. We had only just met, but it was obvious he too wanted to see healing, not only for the injustices suffered by these people, but also by the Catholic Church. "We can't move on until the past is healed," he said.

The following day, he took us on a tour of the island. At its maximum, it is only 14 miles wide and 21 miles long, so it is not large. We started at Codrington College, in the Parish of St John where many of the descendants of the Poor Whites still live. We were introduced to a local doctor who told us that she believed that many of the sicknesses among the population were rooted in the past. Interesting, I thought. Driving through this area helped us to get a good perspective of where and how the people lived, though we did not try to talk to anyone. We were told they are private people and keep themselves to themselves. However, we did meet one lady at St Margaret's, an Anglican Church in Martins Bay. We could hear singing coming from inside and, not wanting to intrude, we looked around the churchyard instead. This, for us, was quite sobering. Most of the graves were marked with just a small white wooden cross. The singing stopped and we returned to the church. A lady appeared who was happy to chat. She told us her name was Anne and she had just been to choir practice. She was happy to have her photograph taken, which made our day. Little did we know then, but this was to be the start of a special relationship.

We carried on around the Atlantic coast and up the hill, where you get a magnificent view of what is locally known as the Scottish district. It was at this point we realised that, although the Irish Catholics were the biggest group to be deported, Scottish people suffered too. Why hadn't we realised this before? We continued our journey to the old plantation house which Sean O'Callaghan mentions in his book;

> *"St Nicholas Abbey, the only stone house built during the period and still occupied, although not by the descendants of the planter who built it. The slave lines have long disappeared and a fine lawn covers the ground where the ancestors of the Red Legs lived in squalor and degradation. How many of them lie buried in unhallowed ground or were thrown into nearby swamps, now filled in?"*

St Margaret, Anglian Church in Martins Bay.

So much of what we saw that day touched us deeply. However, I was unprepared for how the cave near Speightstown would affect me. We were told that this secluded area gave the Catholic people a safe place to celebrate Mass, which was banned at the time. If discovered, the attendees could be killed. Standing in this place, I could sense the fear, as well as the sadness, they would have felt, and also the hope that faith brings.

We wanted to do some more research while in Barbados and so we met with the curator of the museum in Bridgetown. Talking to him, we began to understand how this part of their history had become confused. Even before Cromwell, many came over as indentured servants. Indentured servants had a contract, which gave them the right to complain about conditions and, once they had served their time, they would be given land of their own as payment. We learned too that the museum staff were aware of Irish people being transported to Barbados against their will. They quoted Doctor Micheal O'Siochru, Professor of Modern History at Trinity College, Dublin, Ireland, who has researched Cromwell extensively. In his book, *God's Executioner*, he records how there is irrefutable evidence of the forced transportation of many women and children to work on the sugar plantations of the Caribbean, and of civilians being deliberately targeted. So, not all the settlers were indentured.

As we read the accounts, it was obvious that others had discovered this too. It is also clear the indentured servants didn't have an easy time of it either. Their contract was only rarely honoured and they were often treated appallingly, worse than the slaves even. Historians have battled over this for years, but one thing is certain; they all suffered. We left the museum and headed to the harbour where the new arrivals would have been auctioned. The sea is so blue, it is hard to think that somewhere so beautiful can also hold such terrible memories. In Sean's book, he describes how the deportees were stripped naked, so that buyers could see they were getting good stock. As we stood there, imagining the humiliation they would have felt, I recalled a dream I had the first night we were in Barbados. In the dream, I wanted to take a shower, but the shower had been installed in a bay window. I could not understand why this was. I kept saying 'I can't shower there, everyone will see me.' When I woke the next day, the phrase came to me, 'The injustice is being exposed'.

It had been quite an emotional time, so we were relieved when one afternoon Father Harcourt invited us to attend a wedding ceremony he was conducting. "As the couple come from Ireland," he said, "I thought you might like to join me." We were thrilled, but little did we know that we were also in for a big surprise. The small church was beautiful, a converted cinema, with the turquoise Caribbean Sea visible through the windows on either side of the altar. We felt a little uncomfortable at first, as we were the only guests. However, when the bride and groom arrived, we just looked at each other in utter disbelief. We had spoken to this couple at Gatwick airport! They were on our flight and were getting anxious they had missed their slot to board whilst attending to their young children. We felt privileged to share their joy that afternoon. Even though we had no idea if they would recognise us, we introduced ourselves. Much to our, and Father Harcourt's, amazement, they remembered us and were equally amazed.

We went from there to Independence Square in Bridgetown, for the celebration of National Heroes Day. One hero, the cricketer Sir Garry Sobers, was sat just in front of us. As you would expect, the African slaves were mentioned more than once, and so they should be, but there was no mention of the Whites. Nevertheless, Cromwell was mentioned in a speech of Errol Barrow's which was read. Errol Barrow had led the country to independence in 1966. After the ceremony, Father Harcourt introduced us to the Minister for Culture. I explained to him our reason for being there, but he was adamant that this part of history should be forgotten. He said that he believed the island had moved on. However, I was able to remind him of the speech we had just heard and pointed out that Cromwell had not been forgotten, and neither had the African slaves. He had to agree. Next, to my amazement, we were introduced to the Prime Minister, David Thompson, and his wife. I shared with him the need to recognise these forgotten people. He was very gracious and listened intently. He even thanked me for coming. I felt he had understood our mission, and he asked Father Harcourt to keep him updated. We had prayed that we would be able to speak to people in authority, but I never imagined it would be the Prime Minister!

On our last day on the island, we were invited to visit the Sisters at the Ursuline Convent, which was once a very grand plantation house, but is now a school. As this was where our hostess, Jean, had been educated, she offered to take us. We were met by Sister Theresa Mary and as we were shown around, Jean enjoyed recalling her time there. Sister Theresa Mary was delighted and turned to me saying, "See what you are doing - you are reconnecting us with our history. The Lord is using you to bring us together."

This visit had far exceeded our expectations. We had seen the evidence with our own eyes. We had met people of influence and recognised that Father Harcourt held a huge key. We were now in a position to start planning an official visit later in the year.

CHAPTER 5

I Am Who I Am

Huntingdon Churches Together had been incredibly supportive, so I was delighted when I was invited to share about our trip at their next meeting. They all listened intently as I told how Father Harcourt had opened doors we had not expected. I finished by saying that he planned to visit Huntingdon to see Cromwell's hometown for himself. I could see one minister, Reverend David Busk, was eager to respond and, to my utter amazement, he told everyone that he knew Father Harcourt from his university days. "He is such a lovely guy. If possible, I would love to catch up with him." As he said this, I remembered what Sister Theresa Mary had said a few days before about reconnecting them with their history. Everyone was impressed and agreed that a letter of apology should be written to the people of Barbados. David Busk was the perfect person to do this and he readily accepted the task.

A month later, Vanessa and I caught up with Father Harcourt in Ireland. We travelled down to Wexford, to Father Finn's parish, where many people, including journalists from the local paper, had gathered. Father Harcourt shared not only his Irish ancestry, but also his heart for justice for the Catholic Church and the people in Barbados. You could have heard a pin drop. It was obvious that everyone understood how significant this was. They recognised it wasn't just something that happened centuries ago, but was still affecting people today. Within a day or so, Father Harcourt arrived in Huntingdon. We had kept the planned reunion with David a surprise and his face was a picture when they met up. We were pleased to be able to reconnect them. Father Harcourt also wanted to learn more about our history, so we took him to the Cromwell Museum, as well as the site of the house where Cromwell was born, which is now a nursing home, Cromwell Clinic. Here a copy of the death warrant for King Charles I is on display, so I asked the lady on the desk if we could go in, telling her why. She was extremely interested saying, "I wish we could go back in history and undo all this." It is curious how those outside of the church often grasp what we are doing more quickly.

The summer was flying by and our planned return to Barbados was drawing ever closer. We chose September, as it was the same month the law was passed which enabled more people to be deported. There was little planned for this visit beyond a Reconciliation Service at St Patrick's Catholic Cathedral in Bridgetown. While on a retreat in August, I pondered what we might include in the service. The teaching was based on the woman who washed the feet of Jesus. In the Jewish culture of that day, for the woman to do this, she would be very vulnerable. It inspired me that we too could wash the feet of the people in Barbados. We had to become vulnerable. You cannot be proud and wash feet! She was silent, but her actions spoke louder than words. That is how it must be for us too. We too needed to demonstrate our love for the people.

As the day of our departure approached, I received an email from the then Arise Chaplain, Reverend Scott Watts. He had been praying about our trip and felt God say, "If anyone asks you Shirley why you are there, you are to say 'I AM sent me'." This panicked me as it is not the sort of language I normally use. I knew it came from the story of Moses in the Bible, but not being a theologian, I was not sure I fully understood the 'I AM' part. In any case, how on earth could I say that? Scott shared his thoughts at our commissioning service a few days later and when I got home, I was still struggling with the 'I AM' bit. It sounded too religious. What could it mean? I could not sleep that night as it kept going round and round in my head. In the end,

I got up at 4 am and read again the story of Moses. I could see the similarities. He felt inadequate, so did I. He had no clue what he was going to say, neither had I. I got to the bit where it says, "I am who I am" and I remember saying "I know this means you, God, but I am who I am too. I will do anything as long as I know it's you." At that point, peace came and I was able to return to bed and sleep.

It was early morning when Annette, Vanessa and I arrived at the airport, not knowing what was about to take place. that our minds were about to be blown. Gottfried Bernard, the publisher, had gone to the wrong terminal and we were having problems connecting with him, which was panicking us. Whilst we were waiting, I asked Vanessa to go and see if she could get us a coffee. Within seconds, she returned saying, "You have got to come and see this, Shirley. You are never going to believe it!" She was right. There, across the whole width of the airport terminal, was written in large letters, 'I AM WHO I AM BECAUSE OF EVERYONE'. This was just the confirmation I needed! I didn't fully understand what it meant, but I knew it was there for us to see. I took a photograph because I thought no one would ever believe this.

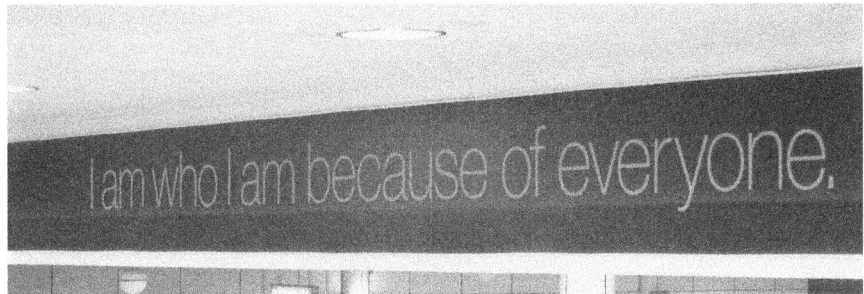

Proof, if proof is needed.

The team for this trip consisted of Annette, Vanessa and myself from Huntingdon, David and Pauline Shirley from the Republic of Ireland, Phyllis Forsythe from Northern Ireland and Gottfried Bernard from Germany. We all arrived in Barbados together and Margaret Butler joined us soon after from Newcastle, England. I had met Margaret after she read my book and got in touch. It transpired that she was married to a Bajan (someone from Barbados) and travelled to the island regularly. She too had a real passion to see justice for the Poor Whites, so we were delighted when she decided to join us. Everyone accompanying me on this trip had come with their own unique story so, at the first team meeting, we all introduced ourselves and shared how we came to be on this trip. It was important for us to get to know each other better. I could see, for instance, that David (the gentleman descended from a Cromwellian soldier) was going to have a very emotional time and each of us needed to understand why, so we could support him.

The Sunday morning service was the first of many opportunities I was given to share about what we were doing on the island ahead of the Reconciliation Service. The cathedral was full and it was hard for me to gauge what the congregation knew, if anything. So, I decided to tell them a little of the background and how we were led to their island. "There's more to tell," I said as I stood down, hoping they would come to hear more. On another occasion when I was sharing, I realised that most people were unaware of how the Poor Whites came to be in Barbados. So, I started with a short history of the English Civil War and the part Cromwell played in this injustice. Throughout my talk, I was conscious of a young man in the congregation getting excited and later he asked if he could speak. He started by saying, very passionately, that he believed this was from God and everyone needed to listen. Another young lady came forward saying how she had had the book *To Hell or Barbados* on her desk all year, waiting to write a review, which was finally written and going out that week. She felt this was God's timing. It was very confirming.

Father Harcourt had arranged for the team to be taken on a tour around the island to visit places of interest. St John's Church made a huge impression, as it stands high on the cliff, with the most magnificent view of the East Coast. Even though we recognised our chances of meeting any descendants were slim, we went down to Martins Bay just to see where they have settled. We drove around the coast and up the hill, which overlooks the area known as Little Scotland. We were told how the people were forced to carry the sugar cane on their backs, up the almost-vertical cliff. It would not have been easy. David, in particular, was deeply affected by hearing these stories. Our next destination was St Nicholas Abbey, where we were shown documents that prove, beyond doubt, that the Whites were considered practically worthless, as the tropical heat and sickness made it difficult for them to work. We also learned why indentured servants were also treated badly - it was because they were only 'rented' not 'owned', as a slave was. When a plantation owner purchased a slave, they became his property, very often taking his surname, and so it was in the owner's interest to look after his investment. When you are only rented, you have no such value.

One appointment we had was with the Minister of Culture. When we met in the Spring, he seemed unconvinced that we should open this wound. However, this time we were in for a surprise. He had recently made a bold comment in the local press, that 'In the 17th Century, Blacks and Whites arrived in Barbados on the same boat'. It had caused quite a stir. Understandably, many descendants of African slaves get offended as they do not believe that White people suffered the same horrific fate as their ancestors. After all, it was White people who did this. I never want to diminish in any way the injustice and dreadful suffering of the African slaves. It was truly appalling. However, I must stay focused on those Cromwell had deported because that's what I am called to do. The Minister listened intently as I explained our desire for justice for all people. He agreed that the truth about the Poor Whites and their descendants needed to be recognised as part of the island's history. We were thrilled, but very aware this would be difficult for him, given the furore his previous comment had caused.

That afternoon Georgina and Stephen arrived from Wexford and they told us they had been upgraded to First Class for their flight.

They felt uneasy about this, like they did not deserve it. We disagreed with them, as it was from their area that many Irish Catholics, like Georgina, were shipped out on slave ships. So, for them to get this special treatment seemed very appropriate. Their timing was perfect too, as they were able to join us that evening for the Reconciliation Service at St Patrick's Catholic Cathedral. Father Harcourt, who has a wonderful singing voice, led us in worship and prayer before handing over to me. I was a little taken aback, as I had thought he would lead the whole service. I didn't have a plan, so I began by reading a letter of greeting from Huntingdon's Member of Parliament, before sharing my story and how I had been led to this moment. Afterward, I invited David Shirley to join me and before he spoke, he removed his shoes, explaining that he was standing on Holy Ground. This was so powerful you could hear a pin drop. He told everyone how we met back in 2002 and the deep effect it had on him, and how he subsequently learned that his forefathers had been part of Cromwell's army. He broke down in tears and kept saying, "I am so deeply sorry. I am so sorry for the way my ancestors treated yours." There was a stillness and peace in the air. This truly was Holy Ground. I too was extremely emotional and it was a while before I could compose myself to read the letter from the Churches in Huntingdon;

> *To the Clergy and people of the Catholic Church in Barbados*
>
> *We, the members of Churches Together in Huntingdon and Godmanchester, England belong to many traditions of Christianity- Catholic, Anglican, Baptist, Methodist, Independent, Quaker and others. We send our sincere greetings in the name of our Lord Jesus Christ to the clergy and people of the Catholic Church in Barbados.*
>
> *Huntingdon is the birthplace of Oliver Cromwell. In the 1650s, Cromwell saw the slave trade as a way of clearing the lands of Ireland, Scotland, Wales and England of Royalist supporters and Catholics. As you*

will know, many thousands of Catholics were shipped out to Barbados as indentured labourers -often to be treated as slaves on arrival - or were transported directly as slaves to work the plantations. All were denied the freedom to practise their Catholic faith. We have become aware that the memory of this cruel persecution remains in your land, as it does in Ireland, and that this story is almost unknown in Cromwell's birthplace and in this country as a whole.

We are all inheritors, for good or ill, of what has gone before. If one group of people has been disadvantaged by history, that disadvantage can last for generations. And we know only too well that resentment or unresolved injustice is one of the most powerful motives of conflict. Equally, if a nation such as ours forgets an act of oppression committed in its name, even by a generation long dead, we make it easier to ignore or even condone oppression in our own time. Conversely, bringing people together in the name of God, whose Spirit is the healing of the nations, can lead to remarkable friendships flowering across divisions, and can offer a sign of hope in a divided world.

We as members of churches in Cromwell's birthplace wish to express our sorrow to you, the spiritual heirs and descendants of those who were oppressed, for what took place. We wholeheartedly and prayerfully support this work of reconciliation. We pray for the healing power of Christ to unite us all in His love, and we pray for God's blessing on your church and all the people of Barbados.

In the name of our Lord and Saviour, Jesus Christ.

To finish, we asked the congregation if they would allow us to wash their feet. One by one, from Father Harcourt to a young girl, they came forward. We finished with the hymn, "*To God be the Glory*" and as we sang the last verse, I turned and saw a fair-haired little girl running down the aisle towards me, with her arms in the air. It was as if she was saying, "Thank you" on behalf of all those little ones from years ago. With tears in my eyes, I picked her up and held her tight. As people left that evening, they lined up to receive their own copy of the letter. Many expressed a deep sense of gratitude and one lady commented, "You are an answer to my prayers."

If we had gone home then, it would have been enough, but we were soon to discover there was more in store. The very next day, Father Harcourt got in touch to say that an appointment had been arranged with the President of the Senate, Doctor Branford Taitt. I felt a little nervous about this, but it is no good praying for opportunities to speak with people in authority, then shying away once the opportunity arises. We were greeted warmly by Doctor Taitt and he showed us around the Lower House of Parliament, pointing out the stained-glass windows depicting English Monarchs through the centuries, even including one of Oliver Cromwell. He led us to the Upper House of the Senate. It is a grand room with a large oval table and a floor-to-ceiling picture of Her Majesty, Queen Elizabeth II. The President of the Senate turned to me and said, "Well, Shirley, tell me why you're here." I had only a few minutes to tell a story that spans many years. He listened intently. With a lump in my throat, I read to him the letter addressed to the Government and People of Barbados, which was largely the same as the one for the churches with the following short addition;

> *We, as Christians here, recognise the pain his legacy has left in many parts of the world, including Barbados. In 2002 we sent a letter to the churches and peoples of Ireland expressing how deeply sorry we were for the pain they had suffered. However, since then, this appalling trade of human lives has come to our attention and we recognise that treating people in this way cannot be justified and is ungodly.*

It was obvious the President was touched. With a tear in his eye and holding me tight, he accepted the letter on behalf of the government and the people. He said that he could not offer forgiveness on behalf of others, but he could for himself. He went on, "As an Anglican and former Chairman of the Synod Assembly, I recognise the importance of forgiveness. I receive this gift of reconciliation. I want you to take back to your city, and to as many as will listen, that someone of importance in government accepts this on behalf of the people of Barbados, in the spirit in which it is given." He ended with a promise that the framed letter would be put in a prominent position and he would do everything in his power to bring relief to the people who still suffer. He also asked for copies of the letter for himself and all the other 55 members of both houses of parliament. He finished by saying, "You are all welcome here in Barbados anytime. You are very welcome!" It could not have gone better!

Shirley presenting letter of apology to the President of the Senate.

In St Patrick's Cathedral on Sunday morning, we saw the more vulnerable side of Father Harcourt. He told everyone how, at the reconciliation service, God had spoken to him about the need to forgive, so he asked me to join him at the front. I had brought with me a padlock and chain and used this opportunity to present it to him. I explained, "The chain represents slavery and the old lock represents the damage and hurt caused in the past, that is still locked away." As a prophetic act, I handed him the small key to the padlock. I went on, "Cromwell had no right to do this to your people and we are so sorry. I give you this key, which represents your freedom." He put the key in the lock and opened it. It was a very poignant moment. Father Harcourt asked me to read the letter and as I did so, he came and put his hand on my shoulder, saying, "We accept and we forgive. Tell your people, we receive the letter in the love it has been given." He invited the other team members to join us at the front and I used the opportunity to speak about the stones which each person had brought from home to represent our lands. Father Harcourt asked us to lay them on the altar and told us later they would be placed in the Cathedral Prayer Garden. Little did I know then where this would lead in the years to come!

Father Harcourt says, "We accept and we forgive. Tell your people, we receive the letter in the love it has been given."

CHAPTER 6

Divine Encounters

Earlier in my story, I shared how we were given a picture of a ruby and the number 40. At first, we felt it was only connected to the publication of the book *From History to Hope*, but increasingly it seemed it was connected to Barbados too, for example, the plane called *Ruby Tuesday*. However, we discovered there is a place in Barbados called 'Ruby.' This could not be a coincidence, but we were unsure what we should do. One thing we knew, if it was important, it would be revealed.

The plane with the name Ruby Tuesday.

One day, as we were travelling around the east side of the island, we got lost, so we stopped to ask for directions. The scenery was stunning and David wanted to take pictures, so he walked ahead along the cliff path. After just a few minutes, David came running towards me excitedly beckoning me to follow him. As I reached the clifftop, I could see it was totally deserted, apart from one gentleman. As he introduced me to him, David said, "Shirley you're never going to believe this, but this gentleman is from Ruby!" The gentleman told me that, like us, he had no intentions of being there that day, but as it was his day off, he decided to visit the coast. I shared what we were doing on the island and he was astounded. He told us that his wife's family were from the Poor White community, but she was too ashamed to tell anyone. It was a big secret. How sad! I wonder how many more people on this island feel this way? He asked me, if his family agreed, could he bring them over to meet us and that was exactly what happened. I told them how I believed God wanted to bring healing and reconciliation to this part of history, including to them and their family. I expressed how sorry I was that her ancestors had suffered and asked her forgiveness for the damage it had done to her and her family. This had a deep impact on her and who knows how many others, because of her testimony.

As we were keen to meet as many people from the Poor White community as possible, we were delighted to receive an invitation to the Living Water prayer breakfast. We knew some of the ladies from this community distributed food parcels to the descendants and we hoped to join them. We were disappointed to learn the distribution had been completed for that month. However, one lady saw how much it meant to us and offered to take us to meet one of the families that afternoon if they were okay with it. We were overjoyed to hear they agreed.

I didn't know what to expect as we drove down into Martins Bay. We knew the people here keep themselves to themselves and the last thing I wanted to do was to cause anyone distress. I need not have worried though, for as soon as we arrived, a couple named Louise and Wilson

Chapter 6 - Divine Encounters

came out to meet us, followed by their daughter and grandchild. They gave us a warm welcome with handshakes and wide smiles that lit up their faces - smiles I will never forget! Louise took hold of both my hands and held them tightly, expressing her joy in meeting us. This was far more than I ever expected. She told us the story her mother had told her, of how the men came over the sea and brought them to this land. Sad though it was, I was pleased to know that she was aware of her history. I didn't want to overwhelm them, so I shared just a little of what we were doing. She clearly understood and told me the suffering of her people had been forgotten. "I'm sorry," I said as I looked into her blue eyes, "but you know, God never forgot you or your ancestors." I thought the letter of apology was one way to express this, so I asked if they would permit me to read it to them. This time, I didn't even try to hold back my tears. Louise took hold of me and hugged me tightly, resting her head on my shoulder, laughing and crying at the same time.

Louise, Shirley and Wilson

I introduced them to David and he too was struggling to hold back his emotion. He said, "I'm sorry, I am so sorry." No words can express how precious this moment was! Before we left, they allowed David and Pauline to pray a blessing over them. Louise was touched and made us promise to return. "We will be back Louise," I promised. This lady was a real gem and I will never forget that beautiful face. Sadly, Louise passed away before I could keep that promise, but 11 years later when I met Wilson again, he remembered that day and that prayer.

Another appointment I had was to speak at a Government Forum. I was told it had been advertised in the Bridgetown press as *"Today's lecture will be given by Mrs Shirley Bowers who will be speaking on the Deportation of the Irish during the 17th Century."* I was horrified! "Oh no," I said, putting my head in my hands, "I don't give lectures." To add to my distress, a reporter arrived with a television camera. As I rose to speak, I knew I had to be honest and tell them, "I know you may be expecting a lecture, but that is not what I do. I am going to tell you the story of why I am here." The questions afterwards revealed they did not want to accept the fact that White people suffered the same as Black. However, I was commended for bringing this into the light. One young lady stood up and spoke. I had spoken to her earlier when she asked me if I had seen and touched 'those people' (her words). She had visibly recoiled when I told her I had. Now she publicly admitted that, to her shame, she had a problem with the Poor White descendants and knew she had to do something about this. She told everyone, "Whether Black or White, to be taken from your land to another country, all suffered and maybe it's time we recognised this. They too are part of this country's history." She went on to say our coming in an act of reconciliation was a courageous gesture and though she couldn't speak for everyone, for herself she said, "I accept your apology, even though you haven't asked me to." She spoke to me again afterwards and concluded, "I think you came here just for me!" The following week, my talk was reported in The Advocate, a national newspaper, and the letter of apology from the churches was printed in full for all to read.

Chapter 6 - Divine Encounters

As our time in Barbados was coming to an end, there was one last thing we wanted to do. We hired a boat and went out onto the Atlantic Ocean, where any slaves who were too sick to sell were thrown overboard. It was beautiful, yet also strange and solemn as we sat in silence, remembering them whilst sharing communion together. It seemed the most appropriate way to end our trip.

At the first opportunity, we went to see Scott and I showed him the picture of the 'I AM WHO I AM BECAUSE OF EVERYONE' across the airport. He was astounded. We have never seen him so lost for words! Scott has always been faithful in praying for us, even though he was unable to come with us. It is risky to pass on a word you believe you have been given, but he took that chance and now he could see the fruit of it. We later learned it was an advertising slogan, but we were in no doubt that it was there for us to see that day!

You can imagine my delight when a couple of months later, I repeatedly read in my Bible notes, the phrase, 'I am who I am'. That name for God had always puzzled me, yet it was this that had confirmed our trip to Barbados. In times past, a name was not just for identification, but also to reflect and express a person's character, personality, and nature. Jesus takes this 'I AM' and gives it a clearer meaning, by using ordinary situations, for example, I am the light of the world, I am the good shepherd, I am the way, the truth and the life. Through Jesus, 'I am', the great name of God, no longer seems so hard to understand. He was illustrating what God is really like. He is light, life, love and truth. He watches over us, like the shepherd watches the sheep. Just like the banner said, "I am who I am because of everyone!"

CHAPTER 7

The Stage is Set

Through the winter, I read the book *History Makers*[9] by Dutch Sheets[10] and William Ford. William, a descendant of an African slave, inherited a cast-iron kettle (cooking pot) along with its story. Slaves were forced to adopt the religion of their owner and if they were caught praying, they would be severely punished or even killed. So, William's ancestors would sneak off at night to the barn, turn the kettle upside down then lie on the floor to pray, lifting it up slightly. The kettle muffled the sound as they cried out for their children's freedom. Dutch and William carried this kettle across America, praying with people of all races and colour who had been affected. William records how he prayed in agreement with their prayers and asked for freedom for future generations too. This made me reflect on Barbados and the need for more understanding and healing. As I did so, a picture formed in my mind of the Arise team gathered in the cave near Speightstown that had previously had such a profound effect on me. I saw us agreeing with the prayers of people centuries ago, as they too were crying out for their homeland and those they loved, for children who had been taken away from them and who they may never see again, that they will one day know freedom, real freedom.

---

[9] History Makers, published by Bethany House Publishers, 2004.
[10] American author and pastor affiliated with the New Apostolic Reformation movement who has written 23 books.

Not long after this revelation, I received a message from an extremely excited David Shirley. He told me that a production company named 'Moondance' were in the process of making a documentary about the Irish slaves in Barbados to be aired on television in Ireland. They had previously made a documentary, *Scotland's Sugar Slaves*, about those transported from Scotland and now wanted to focus on those from Ireland. They had heard about our recent trip and were wanting to interview David. How extraordinary! When we were in Ireland two years ago, sharing *To Hell or Barbados* nobody knew, and very few even wanted to know, anything about this. Now, documentaries are being made, not only about Ireland, but Scotland too.

I am not an historian and I do not claim to be one, but now knowing Scotland held a key to our return to Barbados, I wanted to delve deeper into the history. The first thing that caught my attention was that during the reign of Queen Elizabeth I in the 16th and early 17th Century, a substantial number of Scottish migrated, or were sent, to Ulster, the northern province of Ireland, to own or work the land. I was reminded that back in 2002, when we retraced Cromwell's journey around the Republic of Ireland, we only included the towns where Cromwell himself had been. I was also reminded, that after capturing Drogheda, Cromwell sent 5,000 men north to take the land and secure the ports. Many of those captured would have been Scottish and possibly among those shipped off to Barbados. This injustice and the clear connection between Scotland and Ireland needed to be addressed. That belief became stronger when Mary, one of our friends in Northern Ireland, got in touch. While I was explaining to her how sorry I was to have missed this, she went quiet. I did not understand what was wrong. A day or so later, she telephoned me back to explain that she was of Scottish descent and as I was speaking, she felt both the anger and pain of the past. I told her how sorry I was. She went on "I believe there are many more like me in Northern Ireland."

This definitely needed our attention, but how and when?

Chapter 7 - The Stage is Set

When the Scottish documentary aired, it included the account of the Battle of Dunbar. This made me want to research it further. In 1649, following the execution of Charles I, his son Charles, Prince of Wales was proclaimed his successor in Scotland. Cromwell was disturbed by this and so after his return from Ireland, he set off for Scotland to try to persuade those in power to change their plans. This failed and resulted in the Battle of Dunbar. On September 3, 1650, around 10,000 men were captured by Cromwell and his army. The more severely injured were not considered to be a threat and were released, but around 5,000 men were marched 111 miles south to the English city of Durham. Some were left to work in the mines in Newcastle and many others died en route from exhaustion, malnutrition and sickness. Only 3,000 of them arrived on September 11, 1650, and many of these men were imprisoned in the Cathedral. In the months that followed, conditions were so harsh that only around 1,600 survived and some of them were deported. I felt sick and a sense of shame. Can you imagine the fear in these men, some of whom were only boys, battle-worn and starving? It was clear to me this was too important to ignore, but up till now, no door to Scotland had opened. Nonetheless, with the knowledge that many in Northern Ireland have Scottish ancestry and with our need to address what Cromwell's men had done, we felt Northern Ireland was also important. Conscious that the situation in Northern Ireland was extremely sensitive, even before we put Cromwell in the mix, we knew it was important to seek their permission before we went any further.

For each trip we have undertaken, we had been given exactly the right people and this journey in 2009 was no exception. Our friends, Kelvin and Evaline McCracken, who have Scottish heritage, live not far from Belfast and when they heard of our plans, they were eager to help. Not wanting to waste any time, I flew over a month later to test the water. Kelvin arranged our first meeting at Queen's University Belfast, with a prayer leader from Carrickfergus who I had met many times before and a lady from Coleraine. The lady, an historian/anthropologist, had travelled some distance to find out what this was about. They both listened intently as I shared how we discovered that Northern Ireland suffered under Cromwell too. After I finished speaking, the gentleman turned to ask the lady what she thought. I could not believe my ears. Not only was she quoting the same Bible verses the team had been given before I left Huntingdon, she said she believed this was the right time to address this issue, "Please, please, please come. We need you to come," she pleaded. The gentleman agreed. I have always said that if one person invited us, we would go, and here there were two. As it turned out, they were not the only ones. We went on to meet another church leader, who for many years had worked alongside the marginalised in Belfast. He said he knew beyond doubt that the issue of Cromwell needed to be addressed. He took us for a walk to see how, in recent years, the murals around the city had gradually changed from violence to messages of peace. "However," he said, "one remains unchanged." We were shocked when we saw it for ourselves. It depicted a brutal battle scene with Cromwell and his men and shocking words against the Catholic faith, that I do not want to repeat. My heart sank, but at the same time, it proved this legacy still affects the people and needs to be addressed. We prayed that one day this mural would be replaced with something that will speak of life, not death. I learned a few years later that this has happened. Three beautiful, tall, steel structures have been erected, with the simple yet powerful words; 'Remember, Respect and Resolution'.

When I was interviewed on the radio in Northern Ireland, different opinions emerged. Many people just could not see the need to apologise, as to them Cromwell is a hero, while others knew beyond doubt that this should be addressed. I totally understand the mixed feelings. As I have said before, we are not pro-or anti-Cromwell, we are just dealing with the consequences of his actions.

As a result of this trip, we were sure we needed to return to Northern Ireland to speak to more people, and in the months that followed, we were busy with our preparations. We had a strong feeling that we should make this journey by ferry, via Scotland, as that would have been the route the Scottish people took all those years ago. Days later, as I was sharing this with Isla, a friend from church, her eyes filled with tears. I was totally unaware at the time that her father's family were Scottish

Chapter 7 - The Stage is Set   59

Presbyterian. It was obvious from her response that she was meant to be involved too and I was delighted she agreed to join us.

It was mid-September when Vanessa, Isla and I set out on our long drive north. With sunshine all the way, it looked like we would have a smooth sea crossing. As the ferry was pulling away from the harbour, Vanessa, in a light-hearted way, said "Bye-bye Scotland". To my embarrassment, I instantly started to cry. I could imagine those people centuries ago, leaving their homeland and families behind, and could sense their pain. This was so strong I was unable to speak.

My first invitation to speak was a prayer gathering in Stormont, Northern Ireland's Parliament building. Recognising this was important, we spent the morning in prayer. During this time, Evaline was given a picture of a stage, with blue curtains down the sides and gold across the top, along with the words, 'The stage is set'. We arrived at Stormont and were led to the Senate room. Vanessa and Isla were directed to seats in the balcony and I was taken to the front. From where Vanessa and Isla were sitting, they could see that behind me were blue pillars that looked like curtains with gold across the top - the stage was set! This would become a recurring theme.

The chamber soon filled with people from many different denominations. Margaret, the leader, invited me to share what was on my heart. As this group had been faithfully praying for healing in Ireland for decades, I knew they would understand what I was saying. I concluded by reading the letter, which was the same as for the Republic of Ireland, except for this part;

> Our town has long been associated with Oliver Cromwell, as this is the town where he was born. We recognise the pain his coming to Ireland has meant and still means, **and the legacy of division it has left, particularly in Northern Ireland.** We want to take this opportunity to say how deeply sorry we are for this.........

Margaret responded, "It is important to offer forgiveness. It's not enough to just say 'It's OK'. We need to acknowledge the depth of the pain and the significance of the apology and then respond with forgiveness." This she did. One Catholic lady told me afterwards, 'I have always hated the English, but tonight something has happened. God has done a new thing in me'. I mentioned that the four original letters had been framed and I believed one was going to be presented to an official in Stormont, but I didn't know how this would happen. It wasn't long before we found out.

Preparing for this trip, we recognised it was important to not show political bias. We believe that much of the trouble in Northern Ireland is rooted in what Cromwell did and it has left its mark on everyone's life. So, we were pleased to meet a group of Sinn Féin[11] MLAs (Members of Legislative Assembly) in Stormont. We arrived early and while we were waiting, I was approached by a Church Minister who had heard about our visit. I filled him in as quickly as I could and gave him a book. He asked if I had ever met Iris Robinson, (MLA and wife of Peter Robinson, the then First Minister). When I replied 'No', he asked if I would like to meet her. Of course, I said 'Yes'. However, the meeting that was already arranged with Sinn Féin was my priority. The meeting went well and I was thrilled with the responses. One lady even expressed her appreciation on behalf of her family in Drogheda, saying she was only too aware of the consequences it had left behind in her own grandmother. Time was moving on and as we said our goodbyes, we were sure we had missed Iris Robinson. However, when we entered the main lobby, she was just coming down the central staircase. Because she did not have long, I very quickly shared my story before presenting her with the official framed letter. She was only too pleased to accept it and asked if we could return, as she wanted to hear more, which we did the following week.

The other framed copies of the original letters were earmarked for the heads of the Churches in Northern Ireland; one for the Catholic

---

[11] Sinn Féin is an Irish political party that advocates for the reunification of Ireland.

Cardinal and another for Archbishop Alan Harper, the then head of the Church of Ireland. The archbishop listened attentively as I explained and read the letter, which he described as 'inspiring'. He went on to say how touched he had been and prayed for us before we left. As he had a good working relationship with the Catholic Cardinal in Armagh, he knew he was unavailable at that time, but promised to make sure he received his copy too. We could not have asked for more!

The final letter was left with Ian Bothwell at Darkley, to pass on to the Lord Lieutenant (the Queen's representative in Northern Ireland) who had already been given a copy of my book. Ian is the leader of Crossfire Trust, an organisation working with the broken and marginalised in Crossmaglen, on the border between the Republic and Northern Ireland. Ian invited me to share at the launch of a new venture, appropriately called "Restoring Hope. Healing our wounded past for a hope-filled tomorrow." The banner they had made for this said simply, 'I AM SORRY.' Once again, the stage was set!

More copies of the letter were framed and presented to Bishops, both Catholic and Church of Ireland, the Methodist President, the Presbyterian Moderator, the Lord Mayor of Belfast, as well as other clergy, civic leaders, prayer groups and churches. In Omagh, the priest who received the letter was touched and as he responded, he described it as being 'very weighty'.

I wish I could tell all the stories of the people who touched our lives, but that is not possible as there were so many. I can only share a few. For example, at Clonard Monastery on the Falls Road in Belfast, where the preparations for the Northern Ireland peace talks had taken place, I was given the opportunity to speak at the end of Mass. As I read the letter and came to the words expressing how deeply sorry we were, I was so overcome that my eyes filled with tears, so much so that I could not see and I had to stop reading. Spontaneous applause erupted and filled the packed church. It was extraordinary and I believe it was their way of saying 'We forgive'. Later, I had the opportunity to tell the story in more detail. Here we met a man who had a history of involvement in the IRA (Irish Republican Army), but is now an enthusiastic follower of Christ. He said if we could come back the next week and repeat the evening, he would fill the room with his former IRA friends. To cut a long story short, we did. People came from far and wide and were visibly moved, particularly when I shared the story of the Poor Whites in Barbados. Father Gerry Reynolds, who led the evening, graciously accepted the letter of apology. He said he believed our work was led by the Holy Spirit and he felt moved by the gentle spirit in which we came, the opposite spirit to Cromwell.

We journeyed northwards to a church led by another former IRA member I had met previously. His was a heart-breaking story, but he never once tried to excuse his involvement in the IRA. He did, however, acknowledge that coming to faith in Christ while in prison had saved his life. He told us that many in the church came from the same background. We believe what Cromwell did in Ireland sowed a root of bitterness towards England which could so easily have affected these men. So, we felt privileged to be there. It turned out to be one of the most amazing nights. One lady told us that she had been brought up on terrifying stories of Cromwell and even though she knew that the story had been added to over the years, it had left terrible pictures in her mind. She went on, "But tonight, Shirley, you have turned this upside down." With her hands on her chest and taking a deep breath, she said, "Something has gone from me and I am now free." Another lady told us she had come full of hatred towards the English, but now that has gone, "This is my new birthday" she said."

We finished our trip at the Christian Renewal Centre in Rostrevor, where my son Jonathan came to lead the worship at a celebration. The air was so filled with praise that evening nobody wanted to leave. As we boarded the ferry home, we looked back and a beautiful rainbow filled the sky. It was like a sign of hope. This was confirmed when, a few days later, we heard that a new agreement on unity was to be signed between the Roman Catholic Cardinal and Archbishop Alan Harper. This would take place at Pentecost the following year, at a public event in Armagh and I was invited to take part. Next, came an announcement that one of the Loyalist paramilitary groups was to lay down their arms and seek peace through political means. Real signs of hope!

CHAPTER 8

Planting Hope in a Broken World

Autumn set in and the trees were changing colour. I always feel sad this time of year when the days get shorter and summer is over. My thoughts returned to Barbados and its beautiful sunshine and beaches. We were so thankful for all that had happened there, even though we knew there was more to do. We still had no idea when we would return. However, to my astonishment, I received a letter from the Prime Minister of Barbados, Hon. David Thompson QC, whom I had met briefly on my first visit. He said he had been given information about our work with the descendants of Poor Whites and wanted to know if there was any further word on this. Knowing he had been away during our last visit; I sent him the full report. Less than two weeks later, I received another letter thanking me and saying, "*Keep up the good work*". What an encouragement to know that the Prime Minister of Barbados not only understood but wanted us to continue. I planned to get in touch with him before our next visit, but this was not to be. Sadly, he died suddenly the following year.

More people in our town were beginning to understand how this time in history had affected us. For example, a couple came to talk to me after I had spoken at an historical event in our local church. They had recently returned from a holiday in the west of England, where the owner of the Bed and Breakfast asked if they were Catholics. Strange, they thought, before answering no. The next question was "Where do you come from?" "Huntingdon" was their reply. "Huntingdon," the lady said in a raised voice, "that's where Oliver Cromwell was born. He is the cause of all the problems in Ireland, even today." Strong words, and not ones I agree with. He is not the cause of all the problems, but I believe his actions and religious fervour have left a legacy of pain and anger that is still alive and eats away at people.

As I pondered more on this, I began to ask myself the question; Had religion, with all its rules and laws, affected my life? My father was a deeply religious man who had strong views about keeping the rules and what would happen if you didn't. As a child, I was often told that God was in Heaven with a big black book, writing down everything I did wrong, ready to punish me later. I recognised this had filled me with fear and, although I do not fear in that way anymore, I could see some of what my father instilled in me was still there. I listened to a teaching on the laws written in the Ten Commandments. It explained that God, being a God of love, instead of saying in an angry voice, "*Thou shall not ...*" was actually saying, "*Don't do that. You did it before and look how it messed you up. Don't do it again.*" It was the voice of a loving parent, not someone who ruled by fear. Although this blew my mind, I found it hard to believe. However, I soon came to understand that my perception of God had been moulded, not only by my upbringing, but also through some of the teaching in the church at that time. Realising how this must have affected my children, I asked forgiveness and, at the same time, I forgave my father - he, like me, was only passing on what he had been taught and believed. Cromwell too was a product of his upbringing. His legalistic mindset blinded him from seeing people through God's eyes of love.

I had another trip to Northern Ireland planned in May 2010, but in April, a volcano in Iceland erupted and the fallout of ash caused many flights over Europe to be cancelled or disrupted. In faith, Isla and I booked tickets, praying that the ash cloud wouldn't stop us from going and it didn't. Vanessa followed a few days later.

The first day, we went back to Stormont for another meeting with Sinn Féin members which Phyllis Forsythe had arranged. It was a different group of people from the ones we had met the previous year, but it was not long before we realised how much this meant to them too. Once I had read the letter, there was a look of surprise on their faces, followed by applause. It never ceases to amaze me how powerful this letter is. Job done, I thought. We were led down the marble staircase towards the exit. However, before I knew it, we turned left instead of carrying on. Where were we going? We turned the corner and saw a sign that read, 'Deputy First Minister'. I was stunned, but before I could say anything, the door opened and there stood Martin McGuinness, Deputy First Minister and joint Sinn Fein leader with Gerry Adams, president of Sinn Féin. He stretched out his hand to greet me. I had definitely not expected this! We were shown into a large room and straight away Phyllis spoke up, "This is Shirley Bowers from Huntingdon; Cromwell's birthplace, and she is over here to say sorry for what he did in Ireland." The man looked stunned as he turned to me and said, "Shirley you have nothing to apologise for." "No, I haven't," I replied, "it's not personal, but, like you, I represent people who have." He nodded his head just once. I reminded him of the recent statement he had made about an agreement for Westminster to hand over more power to the Northern Ireland Assembly which the media had called the *Act of Settlement*. I had his attention. I went on to say that in the 17th Century, a previous Act of Settlement had been passed to enable Cromwell to take land from the Irish. "I believe this small symbolic act is a way of giving it back," I said. I asked permission to read the letter of apology and presented it to him. He was touched and, putting his hand on my shoulder, sincerely thanked us for coming. Many years later, I was pleased to hear how, on one of his television broadcasts, the letter could be seen on the wall behind him. It proves how much it meant to him. It is worth saying here, our work is not always easy. It does sometimes upset people and maybe that's you. I totally understand why you might feel this way, but please remember I hadn't asked for this meeting. However, one of my roles is to say sorry for the suffering of anyone's ancestors, including those of the late Martin McGuinness. I would never condone any of his prior actions - he alone was responsible for those. However, I am responsible for mine.

Believing Scotland still held a key, it was very much in my mind and I assumed that would be my next trip. So, I was surprised to receive a further invitation to Northern Ireland, to speak at a gathering in the New Year. Due to Tony's poor health, I dismissed it straight away, though I should have known by then that when God wants something, He makes sure you know it. My calendar that day read 'When you step out in faith, extraordinary things can happen'. I felt I was being nudged to accept this invitation. Thankfully, my son David was living at home at the time and assured me he was more than happy to look after his dad. Soon after I accepted that invitation, I learned that the day before that event, Mary McAleese, then President of Ireland, was to visit Crossfire Trust in Crossmaglen, where my friend Ian Bothwell is the director. He told me he had planned to present her with a copy of my book and the letter himself, but on hearing that I was to be in Northern Ireland, he invited me to make the presentation myself. I had previously tried to get an appointment with her before she finished her term of office, but due to her heavy schedule, my attempts to secure a meeting had failed.

A large crowd gathered that afternoon to hear the President. She praised Crossfire Trust for their many years of faithful service. She spoke of her own personal faith and the need to break down barriers and heal wounds. It was as if God had once more set the stage for me to speak, so I found it easy to explain my journey in a few words. I told everyone that the letter had been presented numerous times, but I always felt there was a piece missing. As the President is the highest authority in Ireland, she was that piece. She smiled and I knew she understood. I asked permission to read it and as I did, I was completely overcome. This gracious lady walked over and embraced me. It was obvious she knew exactly why I was doing this. She accepted the letter with such grace, adding she had read my book and that it had a beautiful spirit within.

A comforting embrace from President of Ireland Mary McAleese.

To my utter amazement, a few weeks later, it was announced that Her Majesty Queen Elizabeth II was to visit the Republic of Ireland for the first time. I read in the national press; "Queen's historic visit will help to heal both our nations, says new Taoiseach[12] Enda Kenny, continued, 'Her Majesty's trip would be a moment of healing that the vast majority of Irish people would welcome wholeheartedly. It is symbolic of the end to years of division and the start of a brand-new relationship.'" Wow, this was huge! The Queen had visited many countries during her reign but never been to our nearest neighbours, the Republic of Ireland. It would be the first visit by a reigning British Monarch since her grandfather, King George V, in 1911. Relationships between the two nations have been very chequered, particularly over the past 100 years as Ireland sought independence from Britain and

---

[12] Prime Minister of Ireland.

the British Crown. In 1937, the office of the President of Ireland was established to replace the British Monarch as their Head of State. Then in 1948, the Irish Parliament passed the Republic of Ireland Act and the link with the Crown was finally broken. It sent shivers down my spine when I realised that Her Majesty had been invited by the President of Ireland. She tells in her memoirs, *Here's the Story*,[13] it was only February that same year, just a few weeks after I had met her, that she decided to press for this State visit. Wow!

We all sat glued to our televisions that day in May 2011. We were completely in awe as we watched the Irish President welcome Her Majesty. It was described in the news as 'The highest tier of reconciliation. A new chapter of close neighbours forming relationship, as those who once were enemies can now be friends.' At the State Banquet in Dublin Castle, President McAleese welcomed Her Majesty and went on to say,

> *"This visit is a culmination of the success of the peace process. It is an acknowledgment that while we cannot change the past, we have chosen to change the future......though the seas between us have often been stormy, we have chosen to build a solid and enduring bridge of friendship between us and to cross it to a new and happier future. Your Majesty, your Royal Highness, it is in that spirit of mutual respect and warm friendship, it is in faith in that future, that I offer you the traditional warm Irish welcome – cead mile failte - one hundred thousand welcomes."*

I was honoured later to receive a copy of this speech.

The President was in for a surprise too, when the Queen stunned everyone by beginning her speech in Irish, "A Uachtarain, agus a chairde" (President and Friends). The President's face was a picture as she turned to others at the table, saying 'Wow' three times. It was an amazing speech in which the Queen talked of their shared pain. However, what really spoke to us was when Her Majesty said, *"With*

---
[13] Here's the Story by Mary McAleese, published by Penguin Ireland, 2020.

the benefit of historical hindsight we can see things which we would wish had been done differently, or not at all." Amazing words that brought us to tears and deeply touched the nation. This is without doubt a clear sign of healing and reconciliation!

I have written to Her Majesty many times about our work and received encouraging replies, so I could not help but wonder if it came up in conversation with the President. We shall never know, but one thing I am sure about - both these ladies believed in the need to reconcile history. I felt I had to write another letter to Her Majesty after this visit. I explained how Cromwell became Lord Protector after the beheading of King Charles I, which enabled him to carry out his campaign in Ireland. I wrote,

> *"Your Majesty, your visit, as Sovereign of our nation, sowed a godly seed back into that land, as you went in the opposite spirit to that of Cromwell. Your humble and gentle spirit conveyed the healing that God is bringing to Ireland."*

I was honoured to receive a reply from Her Majesty, from Balmoral Castle, Scotland. The letter said how touched she was by the sentiments I had expressed and that it had been 'a real source of pleasure and encouragement to both her and the Duke of Edinburgh'. They were most grateful for my thoughtfulness in writing as I did. How amazing!

The following year, we were to discover more to add to this remarkable story. It began when we travelled to Spain. We had known for some time that Cromwell sent Irish soldiers to Spain, as well as to France and Poland. We had no official engagements, just the sense that we could plant a seed of reconciliation. We were astonished to learn that Gerry Adams (Sinn Féin leader) was in Spain at the same time as us. He was there for talks with the Basque Separatists to try to bring about an end to the terrorism in the north of Spain at the same time as we had been praying for those soldiers who most likely would have landed in the north. The icing on the cake came shortly after we had returned home, when it was reported that ETA (the Basque

Separatists) had declared a 'definitive cessation of its armed activity'. It never ceases to amaze me how interlocked this part of history is.

We heard too that Her Majesty the Queen would meet Martin McGuiness when she visited Northern Ireland later that year. This was truly remarkable.

Seeds of healing have become plants of reconciliation.

CHAPTER 9

River of Life

The next few months were particularly challenging for both Vanessa and I so we decided to take a break to attend a conference at Willersley Castle in Derbyshire. It was here that we met Reverend Paul Wilson and, chatting over lunch, we realised that this was no chance meeting. He was so interested that I gave him a copy of *From History to Hope*. A week or so later, to my amazement, Paul contacted me saying he had read the book and believed beyond doubt this work was of God. He passed it on to others to read too. The first person to read it was Jenny, who lives not far from Warrington, in Cheshire. She got in touch as she believed we had something to offer her and her prayer partners. Warrington was the town where, in 1993, an IRA bomb exploded and two young boys lost their lives. I did not want to presume that this was the reason we had been invited, but I decided to dig a little deeper. As Cromwell's legacy is my focus, this was my starting point. His campaign is well-documented and I discovered that he had rested in Warrington, waiting for fresh horses and men, before he continued his march towards Scotland. I was not sure what Jenny's plans were, but it felt right to follow this lead.

I looked again at the map showing the route Cromwell took to get to Scotland. I began to understand that we too needed to travel that same route and visit as many of those places as possible, starting with Warrington. So, on a beautiful autumn morning, we set off for an introductory meeting. Jenny was part of an interdenominational prayer group and as we sat listening to their story, it became obvious that they were not only passionate about their town, but they knew its history and believed we held a key. We were taken to significant sites around the town, including where the bombing took place. A *River of Life* set in the pavement winds its way down the High Street as a memorial, finishing with a sculpture of children's hands. It was extremely moving. We were told that a statue of Cromwell had once stood quite close to here, but has now been relocated. This was too much of a coincidence! This town had given Cromwell shelter, and many were proud of that, but it evoked different emotions in others. We needed to tread carefully.

We sensed we should start by speaking to the civic leaders and after months of prayer, we finally had a breakthrough. A member of the Warrington prayer group informed us that the mayor was holding a clinic in her area and believed that was where we needed to begin. She came with us to see him. As we waited outside his office, our companion announced, "I have something I need to say. I have carried a burden for many years about my family line. You see, I am a direct descendant of one of the founder members of the IRA. I know it was long before the bombings, but I feel so ashamed." My heart went out to her, but this was not the time or the place to continue the conversation. So, after our meeting with the mayor, we went somewhere to talk. "Please don't be ashamed of your family," I told her, "Because, like thousands of others, they were only reacting to what had happened in the past and were standing up for what they believed in. They weren't responsible for the violent direction that some in the movement later took." I went on to ask her forgiveness for Cromwell's actions which had caused such deep pain. She wept. After a while, she felt ready to ask forgiveness for being ashamed of her grandparents and as she did this, she sensed a new freedom. She told us, "Now I feel able to honour their memory, just as I should."

Our meeting with the mayor had gone extremely well and, true to his word, he opened the next door for us. It came two years later, in 2013, with an invitation to share at a Commemoration Service on the 20th anniversary of the bombing. I woke early on that day, knowing it was going to be a difficult one for me. How can I do this justice? Twenty years ago, on March 20, 1993, an IRA bomb exploded in the town centre, killing two young boys and injuring many more. Even though some good has come from this tragedy, the pain is still very real. The service was to be broadcast live and I was the last speaker. I felt very anxious as I walked towards the microphone and could so easily have run away. However, I knew I was doing the right thing when I saw the faces of the people acknowledging my words. I concluded by saying "You have paid the ultimate price for what someone from my town had done to the Irish people centuries ago. I have heard that many of you ask, 'Why Warrington?' and I am not saying this is the only reason, but I believe that because you have this connection and a statue of Cromwell in your town, this could be the reason why. We are so sorry for this. Please would you forgive us?" As we sang the last hymn, a lady came over to me and gave me a hug, saying "You are very brave!" Afterwards, another gentleman told me he had asked the question many times 'Why Warrington?' "Today," he said, "you answered that question and my eyes have been opened!" He and his family were so thankful. Every single one of these people matter.

This was the start of many invitations to places where the Civil War had left its mark, some as a direct result of hearing me speak, others through reading my book. Often when I tell my story, I wonder if people think this is an easy assignment. It can sound like we just pray and straight away something happens. Not so! As you can see from Warrington, it took over two years of visiting, praying, listening and waiting for the right door to open at the right time.

CHAPTER 10

A Connecting Bridge

At the beginning of every year, the team sets time aside to reflect and seek direction. We usually gather locally, but in 2013, we wanted to go away on a retreat. We had all read Roy Godwin's book *The Grace Outpouring* and were inspired by this miraculous story of lives transformed as they encountered grace and healing at Ffald-y-Brenin, a Christian retreat centre in Pembrokeshire, Wales. Roy was the director there and as he once lived near Huntingdon and was educated in the town, we believed this was a clear connection and made it the perfect place for our retreat. I had a feeling there was more to it and felt prompted to take another look at the maps of Cromwell's campaign trail towards Scotland. I was astonished to discover that after leaving London, he and his army travelled west through Wales to Pembroke, before going north to Warrington and then onto Scotland. Therefore, Ffald-y-Brenin in Pembrokeshire was the perfect destination for us and we were able to stop and pray at significant places along the route.

We received more invitations from all over the country that year. Each Civil War site has its own unique story of bloodshed, death and division as families were torn apart; sons fought against fathers, brother against brother. We travelled to many places and I never doubted that every place was important. However, I became increasingly anxious about the promise I had made to Louise to return to Barbados. Knowing Scotland was key, I wondered when that door would open.

It was while we were in Chester that I was encouraged to contact Sue Sinclair, a national prayer leader based in Liverpool, where, it is estimated, nearly three-quarters of the population have Irish roots. It was also one of the major ports used during the slave trade. Within days, we received an invitation to meet her. She listened intently as I told her what we had been doing, but it was the Barbados story that really interested her, especially the Scottish connection. I told her, "We have prayed for years about the need to address the Battle of Dunbar, but we still don't have a clue how it's going to happen. I believe there needs to be a bridge of reconciliation between England and Scotland." To our delight, Sue said she might be able to help and she put us in touch with Anne, a prayer leader in Scotland. Was this what we had been waiting for? Sure enough, a few days later, Anne got in touch with me. As I shared the story, it became obvious that we had a connection and she invited me up to meet with other prayer leaders in Edinburgh later that month.

When the day arrived, I was quite nervous. We arrived at the airport early so I could relax with a coffee and read my Bible notes. The subject at that time was prayer:

> '*Whenever God wants to bring His purpose to pass, He does not act arbitrarily, but touches the hearts of praying people and then ushers in His purposes across a bridge of prayer.*'

There was the bridge I was talking about with Sue Sinclair!

We received a warm welcome in Edinburgh and I realised how important that was, because when Cromwell entered as conqueror; there had been no warm welcome for him. I decided to tell the story in bite-size pieces. This would enable me to keep the main thread, but also give them the opportunity to agree or disagree. Over lunch they admitted that, even though they were aware of the Battle of Dunbar, they had never done anything about it. One of the ladies commented,

"I believe we weren't meant to; it's for such a time as this." They all agreed and were in no doubt that this part of history needed to be addressed and, if possible, that year, 2014, ahead of the forthcoming Independence Referendum on September 18. The battle took place on September 3, so it was suggested that it would be very appropriate to return on that date.

Back home, I refreshed my memory by rereading the account of the battle. As I had read it before, I was not expecting it to affect me the way it did. However, reading the plight of the Scottish prisoners touched me beyond words and I saw of the enormity of what had happened. This battle and all that followed forced a union between Scotland and the Parliament in London, which was sealed on September 3, 1654. It was recorded as the 'Union of Scotland with, and under, England'. Although it only lasted a few years, any union forced by conflict and war is never the union God intends. Keeping this in mind, I was even more certain that I needed to write to the then First Minister, Alex Salmond, explaining our desire to address this issue. It was not long before I received a reply thanking me for informing him of our intentions and wishing us 'a successful and fruitful visit to Dunbar and other locations'. Getting this encouragement from him meant we could continue planning our trip.

Looking again at the Scottish campaign, we read how Cromwell and his men criss-crossed backwards and forwards across the land. How on earth were we going to be able to cover all this? Thankfully, the prayer leaders connected us with key people around Scotland. One such person was Andy. Andy had already read my book and agreed that what we were doing was key to the relationship between Scotland and England. Remarkably, he also knew Reverend Andrew Bain, the Minister from St Anne's Episcopal Church in Dunbar and he contacted him on our behalf. Reverend Bain phoned me, saying that he believed our work was inspired and he would like to help if he could. After a lengthy conversation, he agreed to arrange a service to commemorate the battle in Dunbar on September 3, that year. This was an answer to prayer!

Early in August, we took a break and visited more of the towns and villages that Cromwell and his men travelled through en route to Scotland, including Durham Cathedral. Here, there was a plaque dedicated to those Scottish prisoners who marched south after the Battle of Dunbar who died but whose burial place was unknown. The plaque had been donated by an historian from Dunbar and installed in 2011. We felt we should honour those men and stop there on our way home from Scotland in September. A friend and prayer partner of ours had connections with someone in authority at the Cathedral, so he wrote a letter of introduction. I received a positive reply, informing me that we would be met at the door of the cathedral on September 11, the same date as the men had arrived centuries before, and a service would be held for them in a side chapel. As some prisoners had been left to work the mines in Newcastle we planned to stop there too. Thankfully, one of the Ministers in Huntingdon knew the then Dean of Newcastle Cathedral, the Very Reverend Christopher Dalliston, and we were able to arrange a meeting with him on the same day.

We were as ready as we could be when we set off for Scotland on September 2, 2014. We stopped en route at the border town of Berwick-upon-Tweed. Berwick had played its part in the Civil War as the bridge was one of the main crossing points between England and Scotland. However, it was not until we stood on that old bridge ourselves that we could understand the significance of it. We could imagine the English soldiers crossing over as they went into battle and the Scottish prisoners as they were marched south, not knowing if they would see their families again.

It was a long journey to Dunbar and the day was drawing to its close by the time we arrived. As far as possible, we wanted to follow the pattern we had used in Ireland, to wait outside the town to be invited in. So, Reverend Bain arranged to meet us on the outskirts of Dunbar, at the monument commemorating the battle. We had a brief time of prayer before setting off for his home and a good night's sleep.

Chapter 10 - A Connecting Bridge

I woke early the following morning feeling refreshed after our long drive. The service was a wonderful occasion as ministers of every denomination took part.

Reverend Bain opened our worship with the words;

> *"We're here today commemorating a battle which in many ways seems a very long time ago. And yet the Battle of Dunbar, and indeed all the battles of that war, have echoes of what's happening in our world today. The war between King and Parliament was as much as anything a war about religion, and certainly manifested in that way here in Scotland. Men went into battle with the name of God on their lips and even on their banners, utterly believing that God was on their side and ready to smite down their enemies in God's name. It's not a world away from what's happening now and it shows us starkly how religion can be twisted into something evil when we lose sight of mercy and compassion. In a world where we're daily hearing about hostages, refugees, people driven cruelly far from their homes, we remember those who died on a battlefield that's just walking distance from where we are now, and the fate that lay in store for the 5,000 defeated Scottish soldiers, captured, walked south to Durham, starved on the way, half of them dying on the road and the rest sent into servitude on the plantations of the West Indies. You can only imagine the grief that must have brought such anguish to so many Scottish homes and families. The crying we see from broken-hearted people in Gaza and Iraq and Syria was heard on these streets of ours. So, as we come to pray for healing and forgiveness for the shedding of human blood on the beautiful red earth of East Lothian, so we pray for healing for all the wounds of war: for the historic wounds of the Battle of Dunbar, and for all wars in all times. We have made so many sacrifices, but God tells us through the prophet Micah that He wants only one: "This is the sacrifice I want, says the Lord, that you do justice, love mercy, and walk humbly with your God."*

His words were perfect and once again, the stage was set for me to speak. I was aware that nobody knew who I was and I wanted them to understand this was more than a good idea, it was a God idea. I hoped it would become clear as I shared my story. When I came to read the letter, there was absolute silence in the church. I could feel the emotion rising and I struggled to keep my voice from breaking.

To the people of Dunbar,

We, Arise Ministries, and members of Churches Together in Huntingdon, send our sincere greetings to the people of Dunbar, Scotland.

Our town has long been associated with Oliver Cromwell as it was here that he was born. Arise Ministries has for many years been seeking to bring healing and reconciliation to the Cromwell part of our history.

In 1649, following the execution of King Charles I, his son Charles, Prince of Wales, was proclaimed his successor by Scotland. This came to Cromwell's attention and after his Irish campaign he turned his focus to Scotland. As a result, on September 3, 1650, the Battle of Dunbar came to its conclusion and around 5,000 Scottish soldiers were taken prisoner and marched south to Durham Cathedral. However, only 3,000 arrived on September 11. Some were forced to work the mines at Newcastle and many others died en route. In the months that followed, conditions were so harsh that only about 1,600 survived and they were sold as bonded labour to Virginia and the Caribbean.

When we in Arise Ministries became aware of this, we felt a deep sorrow that someone from our town could be responsible for the suffering of these men. Taking land that isn't yours to take, as well as treating people in this way can never be right, particularly when it is done in the name of Christ. We want you to know how deeply sorry we are for the pain and distress this caused the men, their families and your town. We pray that as we acknowledge what happened, it will help bring healing to this deep wound, and reconciliation to this part of our history.

We, the undersigned, want you to know that we fully support the reconciliation that this visit by Arise Ministries represents. May the Lord bless you and bring you peace and may your lovely land know His abundant blessing.

The letter is signed by all the Ministers in Churches Together Huntingdon and myself.

I presented this to Michael Williams MBE, Lord Lieutenant for East Lothian, who responded by saying

"I am honoured to receive this letter on behalf of the people of Dunbar and East Lothian. I receive it with humility and hope."

We gave everyone their own copy too. One gentleman said that he had listened to many sermons, but he had never been as touched as he was that day.

With the main event behind us, that evening we watched the documentary, *'Barbado'ed: Scotland's Sugar Slaves'* in Barbados. I remember well how deeply this touched Reverend Bain. He said over and over, "These are our kin. These are our kin." I believe that is how it should be and maybe one day, he and others will get to meet their 'long-forgotten brethren'.

We wanted to pray around significant locations in the area connected to the battle and began in the private grounds of Broxmouth House, the site of Cromwell's Mount. It was from here that he is believed to have directed his army. We then climbed Doon Hill, where the Scottish Army camped. It was quite a walk, but worth it for the incredible view! As we stood looking out over the landscape, it wasn't hard to imagine the men, some of whom were only farm labourers, leaving the land to fight for their country. So many suffered, so many died. We wept and I poured oil on the ground as a symbolic sign of restoration and healing.

Doon Hill, where Scottish soldiers camped, I poured oil on the ground as a symbolic sign of restoration and healing.

Within days of the Battle of Dunbar, Cromwell entered Edinburgh. So, we did the same. We went at Andy's invitation as at that time he was working for the Scottish Parliament. He offered to show us around the building, which was interesting. However, Parliament had been suspended because of the upcoming referendum, so we were unable to leave the letter we had prepared for the Government.

Andy did everything he could to arrange appointments for us. One place he felt was important was St Michael's Parish Church, which sits next to the ruins of Linlithgow Palace. Here, they still tell the story of how Cromwell's army sharpened their knives and swords on the stone pillars and stabled their horses inside. However, we had been advised it would not be possible for me to speak there, as it was deemed too politically sensitive in view of the upcoming Independence Referendum. We decided we would go and pray quietly inside the church anyway. As we walked across the road, Andy recognised the Minister and took the opportunity to introduce me. He was interested in what I was saying and after giving him a quick outline, I asked if he would allow me to read him the letter. He agreed and was so moved that he invited me to the service the next day to share with his congregation. He complimented us on what we were doing and spoke about it in his sermon. Around 200 people heard me read the letter of apology and received their own copy that morning.

Andy was delighted we were invited to have tea with Tam Dalyell, a former MP, also known as Sir Thomas Dalyell, 11th Baronet, at his ancestral home, 'The House of the Binns'. Tam, a direct descendant of his namesake, Thomas (Tam) Dalyell, a staunch Royalist who fought against Cromwell, wanted to know all about our visit. I shared as much as I could, including how we came to be doing this, at this particular time. It was clear that both Tam and Kathleen, his lovely wife, understood and he went on to tell us about his ancestor. Kathleen thought what we were doing was wonderful. She said "There should be more done like this, so that there can be a greater unity between us." Tam asked me to read the letter and it was evident that they were both deeply touched. He told me he felt unworthy to receive this apology. "Please don't feel that way," I replied, "just accept it with the love in which it is given." He said he felt very humbled to do so. They promised to hang the letter in the part of the house open to the public, so other people could view it and, at their request, we also left scrolled copies for them to give away. Tam was a well-known Labour MP and had made his mark in UK politics. When he died in 2017, he was greatly mourned and we were thankful to have had the opportunity to meet him.

Shirley with Tam Dalyell, a former MP, also known as Sir Thomas Dalyell, 11th Baronet, at his ancestral home The Binns.

We went to The Palace of Holyroodhouse, the official residence for the Queen. This beautiful place also suffered during the Civil War when it was set on fire during its occupation. Most of the east wing was abandoned afterwards and the remainder used as barracks for the Cromwellian soldiers. Due to protocol, we were unable to leave a letter, so on our return home, I wrote to the Lord Provost in Edinburgh to ask if it was possible for him to receive it on the Queen's behalf. He agreed and the following year, Annette and I were able to take it to his office. I was notified it would be hung in The Palace of Holyroodhouse and Her Majesty would view it on her next visit.

Chapter 10 - A Connecting Bridge

Glasgow Cathedral was another memorable moment. Choirs had gathered that day to practise for a concert, so we were restricted to where we could go, but it lifted our spirits to hear their voices fill the air. On our way out, I went to speak with one of the guides to ask if I could leave a copy of the letter. A lady who worked in the cathedral overheard and said, "I need to hear this." You can imagine our astonishment when she told me that one of her ancestors, a young man of 18, was hanged by the Cromwellians. She even had the last letter he wrote before he died in her bag and pulled it out for us to see. She was exactly the right person to receive our apology and had tears in her eyes as I read it to her. What a privilege it was to know God had met her in this unique way.

I could tell you so many stories like this of people we met in places like Hamilton, Paisley, Lanark, Bannockburn, Kilsyth, Muirhead and Stirling Castle, where they promised that the letter would be hung in a prominent place and the information passed to the guides to become part of their story. At Callendar House, in Falkirk, which had been taken over by Cromwell's troops, the staff were extremely interested and promised to pass the letter on. When we returned home, I received an email from the Archivist saying it had been sent to the National Library of Scotland to be kept in their collection. One of the final places we visited was Greyfriars Churchyard in Edinburgh, where prisoners, including those from the Battle of Dunbar, were held before being deported. It was heart-wrenching as we stood at the gates where they had been imprisoned, possibly without food and not knowing their fate. We met the Clerk of the Presbytery here and he told us he had been reading up on our work. He was interested because Cromwell's troops had camped in his previous church. This really did mean more to him than I had expected. When I read the letter, he replied, "I accept this on behalf of the Church of Scotland in Edinburgh, and all churches, as we are united." It was just what we needed to hear as we started our journey home, calling at Musselburgh and Kelso, before crossing the border into England.

It was the strangest feeling as we journeyed south knowing this was the long road the men had travelled centuries before. We were comfortable in a car, whereas they were on foot, weary, hungry, frightened and without hope. Our next stop was Newcastle, where we met the Dean of the cathedral. He was extremely impressed with what we had done over the years and told us as an historian himself, he too believed that there needed to be healing and forgiveness. When I told him that a letter had been especially prepared for Newcastle, he invited us to stay longer and read it at the Midday Service. Many of the ladies who came were very interested in what they heard and they said afterwards that they were not expecting to have the reaction they did when I read the letter. It touched them deeply. The Dean was also moved and concluded by saying that he believed God was in this.

As we arrived in Durham, we were aware that, for many of those men, this was where their journey ended. Ahead of them was the misery of being locked away, cold and hungry, their fate unknown, many dying one by one. This thought made me shudder and I couldn't get these men out of my mind. I pray, please God, this act of repentance will bring some healing and restoration to the cathedral and these men will never be forgotten. We were welcomed at the cathedral by two Anglican priests and taken to a side chapel where we held a service. As I stood to read the letter of apology, I felt the weight of history all around me and tried not to let it affect me too much. I quote here the relevant part for Durham;

> *On September 11, 1650, only 3,000 prisoners arrived at Durham Cathedral where they were to be imprisoned. We are also aware that of these, only around 1,600 survived the harsh conditions imposed by Cromwell's army, and they were later sold as bonded labour to Virginia and the Caribbean. During this period, the Cathedral's Dean and Chapter were dissolved and worship suppressed, by order of Cromwell.*

> *When we in Arise Ministries became aware of this, we felt a deep sorrow that someone from our town could be responsible, particularly as it was done in the name of Christ. We want you to know how deeply sorry we are for the suffering and pain these men endured, as well as the desecration of your Cathedral.*
>
> *Without doubt, the service you held on September 11, 2011 to dedicate a plaque in memory of these men would have brought healing to this deep wound. Our prayer is that, as we too acknowledge their suffering, this will enable the Lord's healing to continue."*

The Priest received the letter and prayed,

> *"Gracious Father, we gladly accept this token of love and friendship, knowing that it represents a longing and desire for continued grace to undo the hurts of the past. We look to you for continued healing in our lives and commit ourselves to work together for the good of all people. Together we long for the daily renewing grace of God and pray that the stain of our past may continually be transformed by the renewal of our minds.*

Afterwards, we were invited to join them for prayers at the tomb of St Cuthbert. This felt like an extension of the previous service, as the Priest spoke about Arise Ministries and blessed our reconciliation work. This proved to us how much this visit had meant to him.

On our return, I reflected on all that had happened over the two weeks. I was struck by how the right people were in place to make this journey possible. I wish I could tell every story, but I hope it is enough for each of them to know they are an important part of this amazing journey.

CHAPTER 11

Unearthing History

Our Scottish story was to continue the following January when the minister from the Church of Scotland invited me back to Dunbar to take part in a service for the 'Week of Prayer for Christian Unity'. He had been at the service with Reverend Bain the previous year. I was also asked to speak on the Saturday evening, when Annette and I witnessed many people being affected by my story. Interestingly, those most affected were mainly men and particularly when I told them about the people in Barbados. They shared afterwards that they had no knowledge of this cruelty. I had always known the strength of feeling toward Cromwell in Ireland, but had no idea it was how strong it was here until a gentleman called me to one side. He said, "When I told my brother I was coming here tonight, he became very angry. He said I was to have nothing to do with it, as he hated anything to do with the English and Cromwell. However, I am so glad I came, because as you read that letter, I could feel it affecting me and it's opened my eyes to the truth. I thank God for that." I asked if he felt it was appropriate to give his brother a book and a copy of the letter. He replied, "I can't promise he will read it, but I pray that, like me, it will help." Little by little the healing goes on.

We went on to Edinburgh and delivered the Queen's letter, and whilst in the city we decided to visit the Palace of Holyroodhouse for ourselves. We were in for another surprise! Even though we had heard about the gentleman's brother on Saturday evening, we had not come across this anger much in Scotland. However, as we approached the Palace gates, a gentleman asked where we were from. "Huntingdon, Oliver Cromwell's hometown," I replied. He went as though to spit on the ground, and said, "That man is hated here for what he did. I am surprised you own up to it." Shocked, but not surprised, I told him about our work and the letter. He was extremely interested and acknowledged it is a worthwhile cause. "Keep it up!" he said as we left him.

After these two visits to Scotland, we pondered whether it was time to return to Barbados. However, the more we thought about it, the more we realised we were not ready. We were keen to do something to demonstrate how sorry we were, not only in words, but in actions too, and still had no idea what that would look like. We just had to wait and see what inspiration we had. However, in the meantime, something extraordinary came to light.

On September 2, 2014, we travelled north to Dunbar and exactly one year later, on September 2, 2015, it was announced on the national news;

> **"Skeletons found near Durham Cathedral were those of 17th Century Scottish prisoners of war, tests have revealed.**
>
> *Between 17 and 29 sets of remains were found in a mass grave in 2013 during work on a university library.*
>
> *The bodies appeared to have been tipped into ground, all jumbled together and without signs of ceremony.*
>
> *Following detailed study, experts from the university have dated them to 1650, and believe them to be soldiers captured during the Battle of Dunbar.*

Chapter 11 - Unearthing History

> *Dr Andrew Millard, from Durham University's Department of Archaeology, said: "Taking into account the range of detailed scientific evidence we have now, alongside historical evidence from the time, the identification of the bodies as the Scottish soldiers from the Battle of Dunbar is the only plausible explanation."*

Unbelievable! These young men were no longer out of sight and out of mind.

With this incredible discovery, I felt prompted to write to every member of the Scottish Parliament and bring it to their attention. I also enclosed a copy of the letter of apology. I had some positive replies, including one from the then First Minister, Nicola Sturgeon, thanking me for my letter and recognising the value of Christianity in Scotland.

We thought this was the end of this part of our journey. However, little did we know there was far more yet to come as I kept in contact with Durham University, which you will read about later.

CHAPTER 12

Every Life Matters

You probably realise by now this history is intertwined. We cannot separate Ireland from Barbados, or Dunbar from Durham. Yes, we are concentrating our efforts to deal with the pain of those deported, but many others, particularly in Ireland, still suffer the effects of what Cromwell did. We cannot ignore them. This became evident at a meeting we attended in Manchester.

As we introduced ourselves, a gentleman from the Republic of Ireland, made his views known, saying that when he heard the Cromwell link, he felt extremely negative and angry. I didn't want to take over the meeting, but I knew this was too important to ignore. Acknowledging that I understood his distress, I started to share a little of what we had been doing over the years. It soon became obvious that I was hitting the right spot. The bit that impacted him the most was when I said I did not agree with what the IRA had done, but could understand why they would fight to keep their land, as Cromwell had it taken from their ancestors. He interrupted me, saying in an emotional voice, "You have spoken truth, Shirley. You have spoken truth." He went on, "I came here today armed to do battle with you, but I now want you to know that you're my sister in Christ." It was obvious that his pain needed to come out. He wept and said, "This is a new day for me."

It was this chance meeting that held a key to someone else's freedom. A week or two later, I received an email from a gentleman named Ian

Fleming in County Cork, Ireland. He had been given a copy of my book from the previous gentleman. Ian is passionate about unity and, after reading my book, felt led to ask if I would consider speaking at a service for the Week of Prayer for Christian Unity in January. Of course, as always, I was delighted. The more people who hear this the better.

The scenery in Ireland is undoubtedly breath-taking and it lifted our spirits as we journeyed south towards County Cork the following January. At our first meeting, one group had travelled 60 miles just to hear what this was about and told me later that it was definitely worth the effort.

As elsewhere, we wanted to pray at significant sites around the area. Each place is important, but the one that will stay in my memory forever is Glanworth Friary, now a ruin, that stands as a monument to its history. It is well known locally for the sacking by Cromwellian troops and the subsequent transportation of altar boys to Barbados and other Caribbean islands. I asked Ian, as a local man, to invite us in, the opposite to how those soldiers burst in uninvited centuries ago. I felt overwhelmed with sadness as I knelt at the ruins of the altar, silently asking forgiveness for this terrible act. Annette and Ian soon joined me. We were all full of grief and emotion for these innocent victims and their heart-broken families. My sobbing intensified and it was almost unbearable.

Glanworth Friary, where Shirley became full of grief for the innocent victims. Also in the picture is local man Ian Fleming.

I shared this experience at the service the following day and once again, I became emotional. After reading and presenting the letter to the Catholic Priest, we placed the individual rolled-up copies in a basket at the foot of the cross and invited people to come and receive their own. After the service finished, a gentleman named John came up and shook my hand saying, "I just wanted to say 'Thank you'." "You're most welcome," I replied politely. "No," he said more firmly, "you do not understand. I want to say 'Thank you' because this has touched me deeply. You see, I have been angry with Cromwell all my life. It has affected everything I do. But today, through your words and actions, I feel the burden has been lifted." He held onto me as he started to sob. This went deep, very deep. We heard many painful stories that afternoon, of division in families caused by hatred for the English and others who were ashamed because their ancestors came over with Cromwell. The wounds that people carry do not go unnoticed. God wants to bring His healing to all people, no matter what their background.

After my experience at Glenworth and with the faces of those boys in my mind, I was even more determined to return to Barbados. However, it still was not the right time. Tony's health continued to deteriorate and long-distance trips were out of the question. Moreover, it was obvious that there was still more to do in Ireland, as I was invited back to Dublin later that year. So, with the help of family and Tony's encouragement, I was able to fulfil every commitment.

Our friend in Dublin, Doctor Janet Craven, has played a huge role over the years, linking us with key people. On this occasion, it was with the Roman Catholic Archbishop of Dublin and Primate of Ireland. Recognising that he was the most senior Catholic in the Republic of Ireland, we felt honoured to be welcomed at his residence and shown into the library. He listened intently and, like so many, was especially touched by the Barbados story. I finished by asking if I could read the letter and it was evident as I did so, that he understood its significance. Before we left, he prayed a beautiful blessing on us and our ministry.

Every meeting, whether it be with senior church leaders, professors, or someone in the street, is important to us, because everyone matters. One interview I did with the late Luke Verling, a freelance journalist, will always be a highlight for me. He came to interview me for an article to go in VOX, a Christian magazine. I had never met this man before, but I could see he was profoundly affected as I answered his questions. It transpired there was more to meeting Luke than just this interview. He was so impressed with our work that he offered to drive us around Dublin wherever we needed to go. It was on one of those journeys that he told me about his father. "He lives in Youghal," he said, "and he would love to meet you." The place 'Youghal' rang a bell, but it was not until we were back home that the pieces started to come together. In 2007, when my book was first published, I received a letter from a gentleman expressing gratitude for what I had done and inviting me to his town of Youghal. Could this be the same man? His name was Walter, so I emailed Luke straight away, and sure enough, it was his father. You could not make this up!

As VOX magazine is quite trendy, I showed the article to my grandson Ben. He was not only impressed, but understood what I was doing. He had recently moved to London and made friends with a young man from Ireland. When asked where he was from, Ben replied, "Huntingdon." "Isn't that where Oliver Cromwell was born?" the young man asked, spitting on the ground at the same time. He then proceeded to reel off all the reasons why Cromwell is hated in Ireland. I am pleased to say they remained friends, but Ben saw for himself the legacy that this period of history has left behind.

The following year, our attention was again focused on Dublin. Janet arranged another interview, this time with Michael Comyn for RTE, Ireland's national radio broadcaster. Even though I am not keen on being interviewed, I knew this was an opportunity to raise awareness of what happened to those forgotten people in Barbados. Michael was very interested and allowed me to read the letter of apology over the airways so all could hear and understand. He also invited me back once we had visited Barbados.

On arrival at Janet's, we discovered that there was another reason for being back in Dublin - Luke's father, Walter, despite being well into his 80's and spending the winter in the West of Ireland, was coming to Dublin especially to meet me. We were eager to meet him too and recognised that as he was prepared to go to such lengths, this must mean a great deal to him. As he walked through the door, he said with a tear in his eye, "I have waited a long time for this moment. I feel so honoured to meet you." This moved me beyond words as I was the one who felt honoured. Walter, a Catholic, had prayed about the Cromwell issue for many years and believed we were the answer to his prayers. He held my hand tightly, not wanting to let go, as he expressed his feeling of sheer joy. Unfortunately, our time together was far too short, however, we promised to visit Youghal as soon as possible. Little did we know this was going to happen sooner than we thought.

I received an invitation to Cork later that year. As Youghal is in County Cork, we thought this was a golden opportunity to keep that promise to Walter. When we told him, he was thrilled and arranged for us to meet some of his friends. They began by showing us what was left of the priory where Cromwell had made his headquarters and the church where he had stabled his horses. The visit turned out to be more significant than we had imagined and we realised they deserved more time. So, I made a fresh promise to return the following Spring.

Cork was a longer drive than we anticipated, so I was relieved to arrive and see John and others from the Emmaus Men's Fellowship waiting outside the venue. I have told my story many times before, but this time a new emotion caught me. When I got to the part about Barbados and the 'I AM' banner across the airport, I was suddenly overcome with awe that God would do that for me and I found it hard to speak. It happened again when I told the story of Glenworth Friary. At one point, I wondered if I was going to be able to carry on and read the letter, but I did. There was a stillness in the air as John came forward and graciously accepted it and followed with an apology for all the retaliations that had been perpetrated in response to Cromwell. This was an expression of God's kingdom of peace on earth!

In the turbulent times of Cromwell, Catholics in Ireland feared for their lives. To celebrate Mass, they had to find a safe location, usually in the woods, where they could keep a lookout for soldiers and a piece of rock would be used as an altar. These are called a 'Mass Rock' and they can still be found all over Ireland. I had been invited to speak in Milltown, County Kerry, by the group who had travelled miles to hear me speak earlier that year. They took us to the Mass Rock where a Dominican Priest, Father Moriarty, was arrested and later killed by Cromwellian soldiers. Despite its awful history, it was a beautiful and peaceful place.

Knowing this was a Republican area and now being more aware of their history, I wondered how they would react to my story. It was a large gathering that night with around 80 people, mainly men. Some of those present were historians, which made me concerned that they were expecting to hear a historical lecture. Father Joe, a Dominican Prior, from the same Order as Father Moriarty, was present that evening and brought with him the chalice that had been used at the Mass Rock that fateful day. It felt very meaningful as I read and presented him with the letter. He graciously responded by encouraging all to forgive and unite. "We can't change history, but we can change how we respond to it," he said. "We need to follow Jesus' example." I could not get over how much this meant to people, as many expressed their thanks. One gentleman, Liam, had travelled some distance to hear what I had to say and told me, "Lives were touched deeply here tonight, Shirley, including mine."

Hearing these stories, you get a sense of the history and it is easy to understand why this affects people in Ireland and Scotland so much, but here in England, rarely do we come across anyone who appears to still be carrying the anger or pain. However, it is still there. It may not be so easy to detect, but it still needs to be addressed. An opportunity arose when Fiona, a Catholic and the then Chair of Ely Churches Together, got in touch and invited us to join her and others to pray around the city and the cathedral. Ely is not far from Huntingdon and is where Cromwell resided for most of the Civil War. To begin with, we did not understand the full significance of why we were there. However, as time went on, it became clearer. The house where Cromwell lived is open to the public, so we paid a visit. While there, we made another discovery. Some of the Scottish soldiers who had survived imprisonment at Durham were sent south to dig drainage ditches in The Fens around Ely! We were so surprised and even though we were sure this was right; we needed it confirmed. I had kept in touch with the team at Durham University and they confirmed that it was indeed true.

As The Fens are on our doorstep, it was relatively easy to address. The landscape here is very flat and during the winter months, the weather is harsh. We could imagine how hard it must have been for these men, far from home and forced to work in poor conditions. We joined a local church minister to pray on the riverbank in Earith, close to where these Scottish prisoners had been billeted. It was a chilly day and as we stood looking along the river, it felt strange, almost eerie. It was as if those men really were forgotten. As The Fens is a large area, we knew we would be unable to cover it all, so we planned another visit to just the key locations along the riverbank. A few months later, we gathered again to pray in each location, before finishing back in Earith, where we had begun. This time, there was a surprise in store for us - a large notice board had been erected at the exact place where we had prayed before, telling '*The Hidden Story of the Fens*'. The board includes information on Cromwell and the Scottish prisoners. It was extraordinary! Every one of those soldiers is being acknowledged, wherever they had ended up. No longer forgotten, the truth of what happened to them is being revealed, acknowledged and healed.

CHAPTER 13

A Ball of Daisies

Nearly three years since our trip to Scotland and two years since the announcement that the skeletons found in Durham were prisoners from the Battle of Dunbar, we were invited back to Durham to attend a special event to commemorate them. We had been deeply saddened at the way they had been dumped in a pit with so little respect, so were pleased the university were doing this. The day began with a tour of the laboratories. It was fascinating to learn how they were able to confirm beyond doubt that these were the remains of the soldiers from that battle and how they were reconstructing a face from one of the skulls. A plaque was unveiled to mark the site on Palace Green, now in the courtyard of the café, where the remains were discovered. It is mounted on stone quarried from the battle site in Dunbar. The respect and dignity that the university gave these men blew us away - a dignity that was denied them in the past. In the cathedral, the men's ordeal was acknowledged in prayer and the plaque that formally said 'It is unknown where the men were buried', had been updated and was blessed. It was a very moving experience and the day exceeded our expectations from start to finish. We were surprised how many of the project team knew who we were and acknowledged that our work was important. One commented, "Someone has to tell their story."

Our next priority was to keep the promise to Walter and return to Youghal. Cromwell spent a winter resting in this beautiful place, making the Old Priory his headquarters. Although we were unable to go inside as work was being done on the building, Walter arranged for us to visit a private garden in the grounds. The Priory was known as a place of healing and had been a sanctuary for people with leprosy. We were shown many medicine bottles which had been dug up in the garden, proof of its history. As we stood by the ancient wall adjoining the Priory, we thanked God for the compassion shown to those who were treated as outcasts by society.

Later the folk from the local Catholic Church listened in astonishment as I told my story, as did a group of Carmelite nuns who agreed this part of history needed addressing. I was also interviewed on the local radio, when the presenter not only gave me free rein, but once again encouraged me to read the letter over the airways. Some of the listeners came that afternoon to St Mary's Church as they wanted to hear more. One lady, when given a copy of the letter, reacted as if she had been given the crown jewels and another gentleman said as he left the church, "I could feel God's Spirit working here today."

Before leaving Youghal, there was one more place we needed to visit. When Cromwell left Ireland in 1650, he went through a gate at the quayside called 'Water Gate', but it is known locally as 'Cromwell Arch'. We were told it was also from where many deportees had left for Barbados. Years ago, someone said to me, "Cromwell made Ireland sick." As we too were about to depart, we wanted to leave with a different spirit to that of Cromwell and prayed blessing over the town. As we said our goodbyes, a gentleman who had been deeply impacted by the story told us, "There is a chink of light over Youghal now. God is bringing healing to my town." This is how much it means to the Irish people. Every person we met enriched our lives. Thank you Youghal, we will be back.

On our return home, I heard from Durham that the facial reconstruction of the Scottish soldier was complete. It provided a remarkable and poignant opportunity to come face-to-face with one of the young soldiers. He came alive! He had an identity; he was young and looked so sad. This face was to stay with us over the coming months and years. It was as if through this one young man we could see the thousands who had been forgotten.

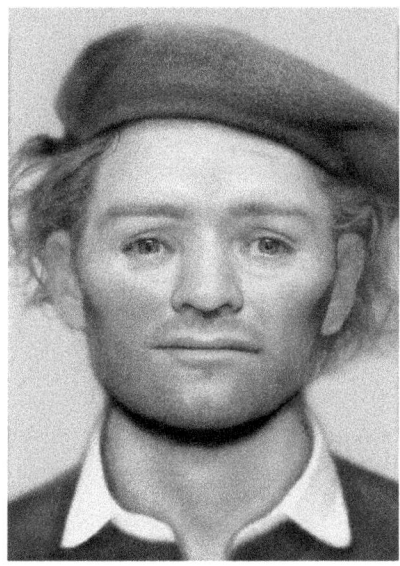

The Scottish Soldier comes to life.[14]

As we gathered together in January 2018, we wondered what the year would bring. We began by reading Psalm 25 from the Passion Translation and verse 4 really spoke to us, "*Lord, direct me throughout my journey, so I can experience your plans for my life. Reveal the life paths that are pleasing to you.*" After a time of worship, Annette shared a vision she had. It was of a ball, rolling down a hill, gathering speed and collecting daisies as it went. It travelled from east to west, before crossing the water. Once it reached land, it started to gather exotic flowers. We had no idea what this could mean. The only thing we sensed was that our ministry was to gather speed and maybe take us west, across the water, maybe to Ireland, Barbados or possibly even America.

---

[14] Facial depiction courtesy of Face Lab at Liverpool John Moores University.

A few years earlier, we had heard Dr Mary Healy, a professor at a Catholic Seminary in Detroit, USA, speak at a Charismatic Conference in Dublin. Mary has been involved in the healing ministry alongside Randy Clark. She opened her talk by saying that she was entitled to be there because of her Irish heritage. I immediately thought I needed to give her a book, and the opportunity came the next day as we were leaving the hall. I didn't have long, but she was most gracious as she listened to what I had to say and thanked me for the book. When she returned home, she emailed me saying; "I did not have a chance to tell you this in our short conversation, but whenever I have heard or witnessed reconciliation between groups in the past, I have never felt it was something I could relate to personally. But, as you were describing your ministry of reconciliation regarding Cromwell, I suddenly felt a sadness well up deep within me that I did not even know existed. Later, I remembered the many times that my Irish-American grandmother had talked about the evils of Cromwell." I kept in touch with Mary after that and this year, 2018, she told me that her parents were in Northern Ireland helping to establish a Catholic College. She suggested that I could perhaps go and meet them there. Wondering where this might lead, Vanessa, Annette and I decided to go.

As we walked through Stansted Airport, Annette, but not Vanessa or I, was given a sample of a perfume called *Daisy*. This seemed important and I said, "I am sure this daisy is just the beginning." Well, as we found out, it was! Airports seem to be a place where we receive a lot of our confirmation and Belfast that day was no exception. As we were walking towards the exit, I heard Vanessa exclaim, "Wow" as she pointed to the floor. We could not believe our eyes –there was a meadow painted on the ground, with daisies all over it! We were sure this visit was significant, but in what way, we had no idea. However, we knew that, if we were right, it would become clear.

Kelvin, once again, organised meetings for us, beginning at Restoration Ministries, where the leader, Reverend Ruth Patterson, asked the question, "What's God been doing to encourage you, Shirley?" "My word" I thought, "where do I begin?" As they knew part of my journey, I began with our trip to Barbados and the plight of the Poor Whites, finishing with the Scottish soldiers. It soon became evident that this story had a deep effect on one of the ladies. "I can see that these stories mirror mine," she said, "as this division was exported to my country in Africa. Depending on where you lived, you became either Irish Catholic or English Protestant." As she continued, it became obvious that there was a far deeper wound connected to her name. She told us, "We were all forced to give up our African name for an English one." she explained. That was it! Like the Poor Whites, they too had been robbed of their identity. I expressed how sorry I was and believed she found some healing. Almost as an afterthought, I shared the story of the ball of daisies and another lady said, "You can collect me on that ball." I was confused. "Why is that, Margaret?" I asked her. She replied, "Because 'Daisy' is another form of 'Margaret'." We were amazed to learn that 'Daisy' is a nickname for 'Margaret', from 'Marguerite', the French version of the name, which is also a name for the oxeye daisy.

It was a beautiful journey north to the hotel where Mary's parents, Nick and Jane, were waiting to welcome us. As Nick is an academic and formerly the President of Ave Maria University, I was expecting to hear about his work and the venture in Northern Ireland, but it was obvious from the start that they wanted to hear my story. Nick opened the conversation, "How do you know my Mary, Shirley?" That was easy to answer! I went on, "I can tell you more of my story if you wish." "Yes, please" Jane quickly replied. I must say that over the next hour, we were amazed by their response and Jane's tears.

We joined them for mid-day Mass, which was held in a small chapel in the hotel. It was a beautiful service and very honouring to us as visitors. Afterwards at lunch, we were joined by the hotel owner, Mairead, and the Priest. Nick was still buzzing from our conversation in the morning and said he wished they too had heard what he described as my 'incredible story'. They were intrigued and this opened the door for me to share. I can still see Mairead's face when I told them of the Poor Whites. She really connected with their pain. I told them about Durham and showed them the reconstructed face of the Scottish prisoner. Once again this affected them both deeply. The priest reached across the table to touch my hand saying, "What you are doing is grace, real grace." I was moved. However, we had another surprise when I asked the hotel owner to remind me of her name. "Mairead" she answered, "it is Irish for Margaret". We started to laugh, and I then had to tell the 'daisy' story. They were astonished. When Nick and Jane returned to America, they told me they had shared the story with as many people as would listen. I began to wonder whether America would be our next big trip.

CHAPTER 14

Birds of Paradise

Things started to move on quickly for us, just as the ball Annette saw rolling down the hill gathered speed. A few days after our return from Northern Ireland, I received an invitation to the re-interment of the remains of the Scottish soldiers in Durham. The university wanted to give the soldiers the dignified re-burial which they had been denied in the 17th Century. These young men were unlikely to be trained soldiers - they were too young, between 13 - 25 years old. I thought of my own sons and how I would feel if this had been their fate. One thing we all knew for sure, was that this young man, whose face we can now see, will always be part of our story.

In May 2018, we joined others for the re-burial. The attendees were all people linked to the men or the project in some way, including civic dignitaries representing the areas where the men hailed from, as well as a representative from their Regiment, who gave them a very moving salute. It was a simple graveside ceremony, held at a private cemetery less than a mile from where the skeletons had been found. A minister standing near me remarked on how he loved the place, "It's like a meadow," he said. Having seen many daisies, we knew this was the perfect place for these young men to be laid to rest. The service and the coffin reflected the traditions of the 17th Century and we were all given the opportunity to scatter a handful of soil into the grave. The soil had been brought down especially from Dunbar. It was a moving and dignified service and we all felt as though we were at the funeral of a close family member. As I stood by the graveside afterwards, I felt overcome with remorse and sadness. Tears came from deep within as I silently said, "Sorry" and promised them, "Your story will forever be told."

It had been ten years since we were in Barbados, but we still had no idea what we could do to make a difference there. We knew the letter of apology was important, but felt there must be more. Somehow, we need to give some respect and value back to those people and maybe a book telling the story would help. My first book was mainly about my healing and how I was led to address the issue of Cromwell in Ireland. A second book could be a follow-on, telling the stories behind those sent to Barbados. However, I felt deep inside there was to be even more. But what?

As Tony's health deteriorated, I was at home more and decided to re-read my old journals. Someone once asked how I remembered it all - the answer is that I keep meticulous journals. It is essential to keep a record of everything that happens and what we believe was being revealed to us. It is no good relying on memory because, unfortunately, we often get it wrong or even add to the tale. It needs to be accurate and able to be authenticated by other members of the team. As I was reading these journals, I was struck by how Joshua instructed twelve men to each pick up a large stone from the bed of the Jordan River and take it across to the other side. It goes on to say, in the future when your children ask what these stones mean, tell them, *"These stones are to be a memorial."*[15] The idea suddenly came into my mind that we too could do what Durham had done and place a memorial stone in Barbados. A memorial that would tell their story. It seemed perfect and I couldn't understand why I hadn't thought of it before!

Over the next few weeks, I reflected on Durham and how they made sure that the young soldiers will be remembered forever. It made me

---
[15] Joshua 4:7b.

think of all those forgotten ones sent to Barbados who were stripped of their rights and dignity. Their faces we will never see, but through this one young man in Durham, they have come to life. Each one was loved by a God who had never forgotten them, nor the injustice they experienced. He had put an ache in my heart for those people; for the children who never played in the fields near their homes again; for the mothers who cried for their missing little ones; for the men, some of whom were promised a better future which never materialised or who died a horrible death. None of them ever saw their homeland again. To every one of their descendants, I promise your story will be told. You will never be forgotten again.

Looking back, it is obvious why we had to wait until after we had been to Scotland and then Durham before returning to Barbados. If not, we would have lost a valuable part of this story and not had the inspiration for the memorial stone. The more we considered the idea, the more we became excited. For too long, the Poor Whites have been treated badly. Even some of their children left the island, never to return. They should never be made to feel ashamed of who they are. As we continued to think about this, the idea became clearer. Many of their forebears had their land taken from them, so we had to be willing to do the opposite. Maybe buy a piece of land and then return it to them once the memorial was in place. We even thought it could include some trees or plants and maybe a seat where they could sit and be proud of their heritage. In 2008, we visited a little church in the Martins Bay area and thought that here would be the perfect place. However, we had not realised how perfect it was until sometime later, when we had a 'eureka' moment remembering the church's name - St Margaret's! You will no doubt recall the significance of the name Margaret because of the vision of a ball gathering daisies and how we discovered that Daisy is a nickname for Margaret. This was the confirmation we needed! However, I must be honest, I was worried as to how we could implement this idea. When and where do we begin? And what about Tony?

Throughout these weeks, we were contemplating another short trip to County Cork to pray at the main ports from where the transportees would have left, then heading west to Schull, an area we had never been to before. This idea began when we heard the sad news that our dear friend, Luke Verling (Walter's son), had passed away and we wanted to mark his life with a small memorial plaque alongside a rose bush in his father's garden. Youghal, where Walter lived, was one of the ports used for transportation, we knew this was the right thing to do. It felt significant to us that roses which represent love, should grow in a place that held so much pain for those shipped out hundreds of years ago.

In mid-September 2018, we gathered to pray ahead of the trip. Vanessa remembered a picture she had a while ago, of Jesus standing on the south-west of Ireland with his arms outstretched. Wondering what else was recorded that day, I got out my old journals. It was in the 2016 Journal, headed 'Praying for the West of Ireland'. Alongside Vanessa's picture, was another - of a crowd of people waiting at the airport to welcome us, people of all ages and going back through the centuries. We were encouraged and felt these pictures were significant.

As the departure date drew close, I was so thankful that Tony was feeling much better and with our son Kevin coming to stay, he was a happy man and so I was happy too. The plan was to start at Youghal, then go on to Kinsale, before staying the next two nights in Skibbereen. Before we left that morning, Vanessa sent us a link to a funny interview with two rowers, the O'Donovan brothers, who became known as 'Boys in green from Skibbereen'.

They had become celebrities after winning a silver medal at the Rio Olympics. On our flight to Cork, we saw a young lady wearing a 'Skibbereen Rowing Club' T-shirt, but did not give it another thought. However, as we left the aircraft, photographers were lining the corridor and we realised that there must have been someone important on our flight. When we reached the terminal, we saw the crowds and TV cameras waiting and the penny dropped - the 'Boys in green from Skibbereen' were on the same flight, on their way home from a competition! Seconds later, they appeared just behind us and the crowds cheered loudly. I got goose bumps all over. It was as if these people were all cheering us, just like the picture we had in 2016. What is more, on the wall behind the boys was a huge poster depicting poor and hungry people back through the centuries, with the words 'Coming Home'. We discovered later it was advertising an exhibition of art depicting the Irish famine, on loan from the United States. Our friend Phyllis was there to meet us. Knowing nothing, she laughingly said, "I thought they were cheering you!"

The first thing we did in Youghal was to purchase a rose bush before meeting up with Walter and his friends. It was wonderful seeing them all again. Over coffee, I took the opportunity to share about the Barbados Memorial Project before going on to explain that we had another reason for being there. Walter was very moved as he accepted the rose bush and read Lukes's plaque. Later, we planted them in his garden. He had tears in his eyes as he said, "You have brought something special into my life." This father and his son had blessed us beyond words and it was with a heavy heart that we had to leave. Little did we know this would be the last time we would see him, as Walter passed away before we were able to return.

It was in Kinsale that things took an unexpected turn. We were walking along by the harbour and I looked across at a stone memorial in a park commemorating Irish Independence. That's the sort of memorial I was thinking of," I said. Vanessa suggested I take a picture of it to help others envisage what I had in mind. As I walked towards it, with my phone poised to take a photo, I received a message from a minister's wife back in Huntingdon. She was in All Saints Church (which is closely connected to Cromwell) with Father Harcourt Blackett from Barbados and he was looking for me! I had been trying to contact Harcourt for some time without success. At that moment, it was as if God had linked Huntingdon, Ireland, Barbados and the memorial stone! We were overcome with awe - it was a God moment.

We continued westwards to meet with Sheena Jolley, a photographer in Schull, who had featured on both the documentaries about the Poor Whites; *Barbado'ed: Scotland's Sugar Slaves* and *The Irish Sugar Slaves of Barbados*. We received a warm welcome and it was not long before we came to appreciate just how critical her role had been in the making of these films. Sheena had spent many years in Barbados building relationships with the Poor White community and gaining their trust. It meant they allowed her to take photographs of them. It was because of her presence that they felt safe to allow the film crew in, for which we are very thankful. We spent a great afternoon listening to her story, as well as her listening to ours. She asked if we had heard Damien Dempsey's song, *To Hell or Barbados,* which he had written after reading Sean O'Callaghan's book. We had not, so she showed us a video of her photographs alongside his song playing. It moved us beyond words, and still does, as the lyrics tell how these people literally went 'to Hell or Barbados'.

Once home it was a quick turnaround, as Annette and I had arranged to meet Father Harcourt at Kings Cross Station, London, the next day. Little did we realise that the next chapter in our story was about to begin. It started in the strangest place, when Annette and I went into the toilets in the restaurant - not the place you might expect! Straight away, Annette spotted a vase of exotic flowers called Birds of Paradise. This reminded us of the daisy story; a ball rolling down a hill gathering daisies, which rolled westward and over the sea, then it picked up exotic flowers. This was so confirming! Harcourt told us he was in the United Kingdom as he was looking to bring people over from Barbados to retrace their roots and follow the Cromwell trail. He turned to me and said, "When are you coming back to Barbados, Shirley?" This was just what we needed to hear and because we had not prompted him in any way, we knew this was meant to be. Plus, the birds of paradise, the exotic flowers we had seen, were surely pointing us toward Barbados. Over lunch, I told him what we had been doing since we had last met, including the vision for the memorial stone. He sat quietly for a while and it was clear he was moved. "This is a holy moment," he said. We agreed.

Chapter 14 - Birds of Paradise

Father Harcourt

CHAPTER 15

Love Never Dies

After the meeting with Harcourt, I felt challenged. Over the past few years, I had not wanted to do any long-distance trips because of Tony's poor health. Now with Barbados looking more likely again, what was I going to do? I realised a decision needed to be made soon. We knew a trip was necessary to share the vision, get permission and maybe even buy a piece of land to put the memorial on. So, if I believed this memorial was of God, and I did, then I had to trust Him. I spoke to Tony about it and despite all my concerns, he was happy for me to go and I arranged for Kevin to come and stay once more.

With flights booked for the end of January, we began to think about a plan of action. Having never done anything like this before, we started to try and work out the practicalities, such as where to get the stone. It was suggested that Barbados would be the easiest and could be arranged while I was there. I was not sure. I needed more clarity on this.

One day, David, our eldest son, came round. As we stood in the kitchen talking about the trip, he said he thought it was a great idea, but he disagreed about the stone. "What do you mean?" I asked him, "It should not be bought in Barbados. It should come from their land of Ireland," he replied. I knew he was right, as that had been my first thought too. We recognised that we were trying to do it the easiest way. Vanessa remembered that back in 2002, we had met a stonemason in

Wexford, Ireland. So, I contacted him and shared the idea. He was delighted to be involved and as his ancestors were immigrants from Wales, we could see he represented both Wales and Ireland. Then, with David's words still ringing in my ears, I had another thought about gathering smaller stone plaques from Scotland, Ireland, England and Wales, each with their country's name engraved. We could embed them in the plinth, so that no matter where the ancestors came from originally, a piece of their land would be represented. Before long, we had stones from Edinburgh in Scotland, Pembrokeshire in Wales, Wexford in Ireland and Ely in England, ready for us to take with us in January.

As the departure date drew close, we were getting excited. However, there was a sad twist to the story. It happened one Sunday evening, January 20, 2019. As usual, Jonathan had come for lunch. Tony had not been particularly well, but this day he had been the best for a long time. While Jonathan and I were dishing up dinner, we were amazed to hear him singing his father's favourite hymn. Normally, this was something he could not do, as it made him too emotional remembering his father. He asked for extra chicken, which was also most unusual and later he stood at the front door counting gulls (long story) and talking to our next-door neighbour. He had had a good day, so good in fact that he encouraged me to go out for an hour that evening with Annette, which was something I had not been able to do for a long time. However, little did I know how much my life was about to change.

When I returned, I could see straight away that Tony had passed away. Paramedics and the police arrived, but nothing could be done. I think he must have waited for me to go out the door. Phoning our children to tell them is one of the hardest things I have ever had to do and those who lived locally came straight round. Once the police were satisfied, they left us alone. We were glad of that. All we wanted to do was sit with Tony. He looked as if he had just gone to sleep watching television, as he had done so many times before. There were many tears, along with a little laughter, as we recalled some of the stories he had told us umpteen times. Our granddaughter Adele summed it up well as she sat holding his hand, "I'm holding his, but he's not squeezing mine anymore." Tony had often spoken of a near-death experience he had many years earlier. He would finish, with tears in his eyes, saying "I shall never be afraid of dying. It is wonderful, so full of indescribable love. It is beyond words."

However that said, I lost the man with whom I had shared 51 years of my life. I felt numb. Everyone deals with grief in their own way and so it was for our family. Jonathan shared some thoughts he had written to his dad. Most of it is personal, but this small portion could apply to anyone:

> *'The sun rises on an altogether different day. Sitting here by your empty chair is hard, but comforting, and the ceaseless memories invoke tears and giggles........ I wish you could have seen the love which gathered here on that inevitable night. Maybe you did, I do not know. Proof, if proof were needed, that you are the source of something amazing - a loving family who knew they would have to say goodbye someday, but always secretly hoping this would never happen.....*
>
> *Legend to many. Dad to few. Hero to me. See you soon, dad. I love you.'*

Tony and Shirley on their wedding day.

Kevin was on holiday in Spain at the time and told me that just before I phoned him, he had posted a picture of Marta, his wife, on Facebook, sitting on steps that went up as far as you could see, with the caption 'Highway to Heaven'. After my call, they went to light a candle in a nearby church and right next to where they were sitting was a candle for St Anthony (Tony's full name was Anthony). "It was meant to be," Marta concluded.

As our departure for Barbados was scheduled only a few days after the funeral, we postponed it rather than cancel it. The family wanted me to go as they thought it would do me good. Val, then a team member, commented, "Going broken with grief means you will identify with those people centuries ago, as they too had lost loved ones." Reluctantly, I agreed and a month later, Annette and I set off.

CHAPTER 16

Honouring the Past

We were welcomed at the airport by Ann Thomson, who we met back in 2008. She had arranged for us to stay with her friend, Nancy Taylor, who, although well in her 80s, was pleased to be able to help. These two ladies have played key roles in our Barbados story and this time it began as we were driving from the airport. We passed near the government building and Ann told us she needed to call in briefly and pick up tickets for the forthcoming Prime Minister's Garden Party. A lady was waiting on the steps and Ann introduced us, saying, "Tell Jessica what you're doing here Shirley." Talk about being thrown into the deep end! I quickly gathered my thoughts and gave her a brief outline. I finished by saying, "It's such a long story, but if you're interested, we could meet and I will tell you more." Well, to my surprise, she was fascinated and as she knew Nancy, we arranged for her to come round for drinks and snacks the following evening. Nancy was thrilled too and told us, "Jessica is quite a lady, as well as being the Prime Minister's Personal Aide." We had only been on the island a few hours and already we were meeting people connected to high places!

Jessica is a very vivacious lady and as soon as she arrived, it was clear she had not come for the food. She just wanted to hear the story. She listened intently and asked lots of questions. As I shared some of the stories, she was blown away. She totally understood and was amazed, especially with the daisy/bird of paradise story and how that had led us back to Barbados. When I told her about the memorial and showed her the stones we had brought with us, she became extremely excited. She was certain that this part of their history needed to be addressed. She told us, "History - the good and the bad - is real and we cannot deny it. We must face it and acknowledge it, in order to bring justice to the descendants of Poor Whites." Immediately she got on the phone and spoke to Canon Mayers, the Minister for St John's and St Margaret's Churches and arranged a meeting for Saturday morning. What a gem! Before we ate, Jessica prayed the most incredible prayer - it was as if she had been at all our prayer meetings. At this point, Ann arrived to give Nancy her ticket for the garden party. Jessica explained that each table was named after a flower and she asked Ann if she knew which table she would be sitting at. "No," came the reply, so Jessica looked it up for her. I can still see Jessica's face now as she gasped with astonishment, for Ann's table was named 'Bird of Paradise'. From that moment on we all knew this was meant to be.

In preparation for the meeting on Saturday, Annette and I decided to see if we could find our way to St Margaret's Church. Even though the island is small, this was no easy task - the roads are not great and there are very few signposts. After getting lost umpteen times and going around in circles, we eventually arrived, promising ourselves that on the next trip we would bring a sat-nav! However, it was great to be back and to see the church looking just as we remembered it, with a small, well-kept garden and a new path. We both felt this was exactly the right location for the memorial. All we had to do was get permission!

Barbados is divided into parishes and St Margaret's is in the parish of St John, with its rugged Atlantic coastline and stunning scenery. St John's Parish Church is situated high on the cliff overlooking Martins Bay, where you find St Margaret's Church and where many of the Poor Whites settled. Thanks to Ann, we did not get lost this time and arrived just before Canon Mayers, Jessica, and Charles Griffith, the Member of Parliament for St John.

As we sat down, Canon Mayers told us that he knew of Arise Ministries through Harcourt and he had read my book. It was great to know that the foundation had been laid. I told him about Scotland, Durham and how the idea of the memorial stone came into being. He became noticeably quiet and we wondered what he was thinking. He told us it was a revelation, as he had never connected the Scottish District in Barbados to Scotland. With real excitement in his voice, he exclaimed, "I know just where the memorial could go! In front of St Margaret's Church are the ruins of an old plantation windmill. As it is part of the same story, it could be incorporated with this." Annette and I could not believe what we were hearing and the more we talked, the more animated he became. "For years, people have been telling me that something needed to be done for these descendants, but nobody had any ideas. Until now! I believe this will give them a real sense of worth." As the letter of apology had been updated to include the Scottish soldiers, I asked permission to read it. It was powerful. Canon Mayers sat a while before he asked if I would like to speak in the service at St Margaret's Church the following day. I readily accepted; this was exactly what we hoped for! We knew it was important to get permission from the leaders, but it was also important to find out what the people themselves thought of the idea. How wonderful to have this opportunity to share the vision and hopefully, read the letter of apology.

The ruins of the old plantation mill at St Margaret's Church.

We arrived at the church the following day and the choir were standing outside. We recognised Anne, the descendant we had met in 2008. Reverend Father Taitt, who was leading the service, welcomed us and it seemed that he already knew about our mission. The service was inspirational and fitted well with what I would be saying. As I stood at the lectern, I turned to Anne and smiled, acknowledging we had met many years ago, before sharing the story of why we were there. I finished by reading the letter, which was received with applause. Reverend. Father Taitt rose to his feet and commended us for our work and vision. He encouraged everyone to get involved. It warmed my heart to see people queuing to take a book and a copy of the letter afterwards. As we were about to leave, Anne approached me to say how sorry she was not to have recognised us. So as not to embarrass her anymore, I asked her to remind me of her name. "Margaret," she responded. Well, you could have knocked me down with a feather. I was not expecting that! "Oh, I thought your name was Anne," I replied, "No, everyone calls me Anne, but my real name is Margaret." She did not have to tell me that, she could have just said Anne. I knew that this was clear confirmation that we were in the right place and she was the right person. As a result, this special lady will always be known to us as Margaret Anne, so that's what I call her in this story. Another of the ladies told me her great-grandfather, who once lived across the road from the church, was of Irish descent. She agreed that the memorial would play a significant role in their healing. Our final piece of confirmation, if we needed it, came on our last day. Annette looked up the weather in Bridgetown on the Met Office webpage and the image for that day was of daisies on a hill. You couldn't make it up!

Back home again, I received a message from Jessica. She informed me that the Prime Minister of Barbados, Mia Mottley, was to speak at a reception in London and she wondered if we would like to attend. Of course we did! It was an honour to hear her passion for her nation as she outlined her vision. This included the east side of the island where, she said 'The poor have suffered enough. It is time their needs are met.' Her heart for this land and its people was just what we needed to hear. I knew it was time to write to her with our plans. Her reply really encouraged us;

"On behalf of Prime Minister, the Hon. Mia Amor Mottley, I compliment you and your colleagues in Arise Ministries for the excellent work you have embarked on to symbolically set right a centuries-old injustice that was visited on the ancestors of a segment of Barbadians known as Poor Whites. The Prime Minister wishes me to indicate to you that she fully supports your plan to visit Barbados later this year to lay a memorial stone on the grounds of the St Margaret's Anglican Church in St John, the parish in which many of these Barbadians of Irish descent have settled.

Again, on behalf of Prime Minister Mottley, God's blessing on you and your partners at Arise Ministries as you press ahead on your mission for justice."

Even though our heads were buzzing with ideas, we were under no illusion that this memorial project was going to be an easy task. For a start, we were waiting on permission from the Barbados Church Authorities and in the meantime, Canon Mayers approached people to help with the design. I was delighted later to receive a rough sketch from him. The plan was to follow the footprint of the outer wall of the windmill with planters and seating. The memorial stone would be set on a plinth inside the circle, in front of what remains of the wall. This was a far bigger project than we had envisaged, but it was part of the plantation story. St Margaret's Church is built on the site of a 17th Century hot house (or boiler house), where the juice from the sugarcane was boiled to produce raw sugar. So, it seemed fitting that we honour the people in a place that is part of their story. The truth of this part of history has been distorted and those descendants from the Poor White community have been misunderstood. We hope this memorial stone will play a key role in putting this right and enable everyone to know the truth. The vision for a 'Circle of Remembrance' was born.

As I was talking with Annette one evening, I suddenly remembered that, when we went to Barbados in 2008, everyone took a stone to represent their land. Father Harcourt had placed them in the cathedral prayer garden. It was a strange thought to have at that moment, but Annette pointed out that when we took those stones in 2008, it was like a prophetic act as they were placed in a garden. Now, all these years on, the memorial stone was also to be placed in a garden. It was so simple, yet so profound! It was sometime later that I came to realise how profound her words were. I was reading again the story that first inspired me to build the memorial, how Joshua instructed 12 men to pick up 12 large stones from the river Jordan and use them to build a permanent memorial. In The Message translation, it says this happened at 'The Gilgan (The Circle)'. Wow!

At the end of his book *To Hell or Barbados*, Sean O'Callaghan writes,

> "*It is my fervent hope that Catholic families in Ireland......will band together and do something for their long-forgotten brethren - the Red Legs of Barbados.*"

I honestly believe that people in Ireland are not ignoring his plea - they are just totally unaware of it. So, with that in mind I, along with friends from Northern Ireland, attended the Catholic Charismatic Conference in Dublin. I hoped I may get the chance to talk to a few people about this. That opportunity arose when possibly hearing my English accent, two ladies asked where I was from. When I replied, "Huntingdon, Cromwell's birthplace," they wanted to hear more. I shared just a small part of the story, including about the descendants in Barbados, and it touched a deep wound. One lady told me that when researching her ancestry, she had discovered the painful truth of what happened to members of her family during Cromwell's time. I asked if they would allow me to read the letter of apology and as I did, the flood gates opened and they both wept. The second lady had no idea at the time why she was weeping, she just felt a deep, deep grief. She believed that what I shared had something to do with her ancestors. "If this is how the truth affects you," I said, "imagine what it could do for others here."

Remaining conscious of Sean's plea, we decided we wanted to give people from every country, of any religious denomination or none, the opportunity to be part of the healing. Not everyone can go to Barbados but, through helping to fund this memorial, we could show the descendants that they are no longer a forgotten people. This was not an easy decision for us, as in over 20 years of ministry, we had never asked for donations for our work before. We never want money to become the issue. However, this was different. It was not for us; it was for the people in Barbados. This memorial needed to come from the people of the lands from which they were taken. This was confirmed when Mary, from Northern Ireland, phoned me and said, "They left with nothing and nearly 400 years later, some still have nothing. They are my people and I want to give." Many others agreed and the money came in.

With fundraising underway and the stone commissioned from Ireland, we realised it was time to return to Barbados to share more of the vision. So, we arranged a trip for October. As we gathered to pray ahead of our trip, we read Romans 9:25-26 from the new Passion Translation;

> *"To those who were rejected and not my people, I will say to them: 'You are mine.' And to those who were unloved I will say: 'You are my darling"…..In the place where they were told, 'You are nobody', this will be the very place where they will be renamed 'Children of the living God'."*

This was first recorded by the prophet Hosea about seven hundred years before Jesus and tells of God's promise of restoration. Centuries later, Paul quoted it in Romans as he believed it applied to people of his day too. Now we felt the same. This was for the descendants and their ancestors.

What a wonderful promise to carry with us to Barbados!

CHAPTER 17

The Descendants

When Annette and I arrived in Barbados, the weather was extremely hot and humid and it did not let up day or night. This was quite a challenge and it helped us better appreciate how much those people must have suffered. Like us, they were not used to the blazing sun, but they had no shelter, no fans, no showers to cool them, no insect repellent or comfortable bed to sleep on. They did not have the right clothes and probably no shoes, and that is just for starters. So, even though the mosquito bites and heat made us extremely uncomfortable, this was nothing compared to their plight.

In advance of this trip, I had been in contact with Bishop Maxwell and made an appointment to see him and Archdeacon Eric Lynch. As they already knew of the project through Canon Mayers, I shared in detail how it came about and after a while, the bishop expressed his excitement. I continued to tell more of the story and finished by saying we believed it was of God, but they needed to discern this for themselves. The bishop quickly responded, "There is no need. I know this is God. That is why I am excited." It was so important to have their endorsement.

Next, we needed the support of the descendants themselves. With that in mind, we headed back to Martins Bay, hoping that we might bump into Margaret Anne. However, much to our disappointment, it became evident that this was not going to be so easy. It is hard to describe, but it is as though the people are hidden in little pockets and unless you know where they live, you stand little chance of finding them. So, we made our way along the coast, stopping for refreshments. A young lady working in the shop asked, "How long are you on holiday for?" Explaining that we were not on holiday, I told her what we were doing on the island and how we were hoping to meet one or two descendants. "My grandad, Fred Watson, is a direct descendant," she said excitedly, "in fact at 94 he is the oldest one left. Would you like to meet him? I know he would love to meet you." This was perfect! We were delighted and arranged a meeting the following day when we would be back at St Margaret's Church.

We set off the next morning in excited anticipation of what the day would bring. We were met at the windmill ruin by Canon Mayers and others, including the contractor who had been taken on to do the work. Being back here and seeing the area for ourselves made it easier to imagine what we might achieve. Margaret Anne and her husband Herbert play a significant role in the life of the church, and they were there that day too. Even though he is a Black Bajan, Herbert has Irish ancestors, so I wanted to know what they both thought of the idea. Margaret Anne flung her arms around me, saying, "We are very happy Shirley. Very happy." This was what we wanted to hear! When the business was concluded, I asked her if she knew Fred Watson and to our delight, she did. "He doesn't live far from here," she explained, "but I do not think you will find it on your own. If you like, we will come with you." We had been concerned that Fred might feel overwhelmed or embarrassed by two unknown English ladies appearing at his door, but having Herbert and Margaret Anne with us undoubtedly helped. Fred warmly welcomed us into his little house. It was evident from the start that this gentleman would leave an indelible mark on our lives. "I love my fishing," he said, pointing to the nets laying on the floor, "that's what keeps me going." Despite being in his nineties, he boasted that, apart from having his appendix out, he had not been ill since the 1940s! He wanted to show us what he called 'his precious things,' including his Barbados Service Medal, a commendation from

Queen Elizabeth II for his service to the fishing industry. Beside him, on the kitchen table, was his Bible and on the wall, an old tapestry of the Last Supper of Christ. He had lots of stories to tell and we could have sat listening to him all day. He sat quietly nodding as I recounted our story and the proposed memorial. I read to him the letter of apology, concluding, "I am sorry that 'man' has forgotten you over the years, but you see Fred, God never did." As we left, he had a tear in his eye and made us promise to come and see him again.

Fred Watson

Margaret Anne and Herbert invited us to their home, where many of their extended family live under one roof. We met Justin, their son, who told us how he loved history and was delighted to hear we were addressing this issue. "It's been hidden for too long," he said. We felt sure he would take a great interest as the project progressed. Just behind their house lives Margaret Anne's sister Hazel, who, I must admit, enjoyed a good laugh at my expense when I fell backwards off the wall we were sitting on! I was under no illusions as I talked with her that she would soon tell me if she did not agree. However, she was impressed and said she would like to read my book. Margaret Anne was in tears and I realised she had not heard much of the story herself until then. As we headed home, Annette and I concluded that this day in 'The Bay' had been better than we could have imagined.

It felt strange being in Barbados for my wedding anniversary, the first since Tony had died. My children, realising it was going to be tough, encouraged me to do something to mark the day. So, Annette and I decided to take a day off and visit Hunte's Gardens. As Tony adored gardening and took immense pride in his own, it felt an appropriate way to mark the day. We had no idea what to expect. I imagined a very English-style garden, but I could not have been more wrong! As you walk through the gates, it is like entering another world. Classical music plays throughout this spectacular garden, which was once the working part of a plantation and was created in a sink hole. Steps and paths branch out in different directions, taking you on a journey of discovery of exotic plants and flowers, whilst monkeys play in the trees towering above you. Hummingbirds and butterflies were among the unexpected joys we encountered, as were the many secret seating areas tucked away at various points where you can stop, picnic and generally soak up the peace. I had a few tears as I thought of how much Tony would have loved this place and wished I could have shared it with him. However, I realised he is now in the best garden ever!

Finally, we climbed up to Mr Hunte's veranda, which had been converted from the old stables, where visitors were invited to join him for refreshments. As we looked around, I overheard him say how his ancestors had come over in the 17th Century. I wanted to know more, so when I saw him going into the back room, I approached and quietly asked, "Did I hear you say your ancestors came over as plantation owners?" He leaned towards me and whispered, "No, indentured servants". I knew that this was no coincidence. He invited us to join him for a drink and asked why I had asked him that question. Well, that opened the door! He was so fascinated by the story that he began to phone his friends to come and join us so they could hear it too.

What we thought would be a quick chat turned out to be over two hours! One friend of his was Irish-American, another had ancestors who were Poor Whites on one side and plantation owners the other. They were both amazed at my story. As I read and presented them each with a letter, Mr Hunte was overcome and said he felt privileged to receive it. Later, when I realised Mr Hunte's Christian name was Anthony, the same as my husband, I knew in my heart that God had blessed this day. Later, as we were writing up our notes, Annette was reminded of her vision of the ball collecting first daisies, then exotic flowers. "Well, today we had them in abundance!" she said.

Despite her age, Nancy is an amazing hostess and she invited Dr Karl Watson, an historian and university lecturer, over one evening. Karl has written about the Poor Whites and features on the documentaries. His words, 'Whether a black back or a white back, the whip cuts and they all suffer in the same way' had greatly impacted me. He himself is a Poor White and we were keen to hear more of his story. He had a wealth of knowledge, but it was his personal experience that most interested us. He described his boyhood home as a little chattel house with no electricity, no running water, a dirt floor in the kitchen and a pit toilet in the back yard. "It was a hard life," he said, "and a big racial divide. You see you are not supposed to be poor and white. White people are rich, so you do not fit into that category. You are not black, so you do not fit there either." He recalled the taunts from his childhood ridiculing him and his family. One memory was of playing outside with his friends when they all ran into the friend's house, beckoning him to follow. The mum immediately stood with her arms out wide to physically prevent him from entering. He was only allowed to enter through the back door. We were speechless and I could have wept as he told us this story.

After Karl's visit, Nancy researched her family line and discovered she too is a descendant. Her cousin, who had helped compile their family tree, came to see us and she told us that her ancestors came from Scotland in 1650, quite possibly as a result of the Battle of Dunbar.

We became even more aware of how many people are connected to this history when Jessica came to lunch. It was great seeing her and, once again, you could see the cogs whirring in her mind as we ate and talked. She so wanted to get people on board and straightaway got on her mobile phone and texted a businessman she knew. He came back almost immediately with a long story of how he had been told that his ancestors were sent from Wales in the 17th Century. I was so pleased we had included Wales in the memorial stone. We believed many Welshmen had fought alongside the Irish and would most likely have been shipped out with them too, but we had found no proof. I later read, in *To Hell or Barbados*, how Sean discovered a survey from 1650 in the Barbados Museum. The survey revealed the first evidence of white men being shipped to Barbados were from Wales and were sold for a shilling each in May 1648. I had prayed for this confirmation and now I had it!

We had been in Barbados for nearly two weeks and spent most of that time driving backwards and forwards to the East Coast. We knew organising the memorial was one of the main reasons for coming over, but our hearts' desire was still to meet more people. So, we were delighted when Margaret Anne invited us to St John's Bazaar, to meet Frank, originally from England and his wife Dorothy, from Uganda. They were both keen supporters of St John's Church and took us on a tour. Dorothy had read about the memorial plans in the newspaper and as we sat under the shade of the trees, she wanted to know more. After a while, a friend of theirs came by and stopped to talk. Dorothy was so inspired by then that she wanted me to share the story with her friend too. Within a few minutes of me speaking, tears started to appear, "Why am I crying like this?" the friend said. She told us that her late husband was an 'O'Neil' - an Irish surname, so it started to make sense. She went on, "I am not a church person, but I am fascinated by this story and desperately want to know more. "Here's my book if you're interested," I said, holding out the copy I had in my hand, "it might help you understand your husband's history." She left a happy lady and I hope, one day, we will meet again.

Chapter 17 - The Descendants

There was one more person I was desperate to see in Barbados - Wilson, Louise's husband. I felt I owed him an explanation as to why it had taken so long for us to return. We had been so careful not to come over as pushy, but now we felt we had to give it another go to try to find where he lived. I mentioned it to Margaret Anne and without hesitation, she said she would take us. This is a tight-knit community, so I should have realised she would know him. As we pulled up, I recognised their little house. Wilson was staring out of the window and our hearts went out to him. He looked so sad. "I miss her so much," he said, showing us Louise's picture. "She had such a wonderful smile, which I have never forgotten," I said. "I promised her that we would return, but I am so sorry it has taken so long." "I remember," he replied, "and that man who prayed for us." My goodness, that had been over ten years ago and yet he clearly remembered it. We were touched. This man just accepted us and did not even question why it had been so long. When I told him of our plans for a memorial, he loved the idea and said he would come when it was finished. We left promising to see him on our next visit. "It won't be ten years this time," I assured him and he smiled, which was good to see.

This trip had such an impact on us that we felt even more committed to what we were doing. Yes, it was costly in many ways, but not as costly as the price those people paid long ago. Now that we had the support of officials and descendants in Barbados, we knew it was time to raise the profile of the project in our hometown of Huntingdon. We began by meeting with the town mayor, who understood and found the story fascinating. In turn, he arranged a meeting with the Curator of the Cromwell Museum. I was apprehensive about this meeting, as I assumed that he would disagree with what we were doing. I could not have been more wrong. He had recently visited Ireland and told us how discovering more of Cromwell's actions there had affected him deeply. "My job isn't to promote Cromwell," he said, "it is just to tell his story. So, what happened in Ireland, addressing the myths and the truths, are now included in the museum." He concluded, "I commend you for your work. Keep it up!"

These meetings seemed to open the way for more, including one in London with the High Commissioner of Barbados, His Excellency Milton Innis. It was good timing, as we were planning to return to the island to check the progress of the project and to personally invite as many descendants as possible to the dedication ceremony. Milton appreciated what we were doing and said, if possible, he would love to attend the event too.

I began to realise that we needed to publicise the project even more, so I gave Jonathan the task of producing a video to tell the story. It wasn't long before he had gathered all the information he needed and the 'Barbados Memorial Project Circle of Remembrance 2020' video was released on YouTube. The response to the video was very positive. Sheena Jolley, the professional photographer from Schull, who we met in 2018, was one who responded. As she knew many of the descendants in Barbados and has written extensively on their plight, I asked her if she would be willing to accompany us on our next trip. She agreed and said she would be happy to introduce us to the people she knew. So, with this promise, Vanessa and I set off for Barbados early in 2020 with great anticipation.

CHAPTER 18

Coming Home

It felt good to be back as we turned into the close where Nancy lives and saw her waiting for us. This was only my third visit, but I felt like I had come home! Nancy was family and to see her face light up, I knew she felt the same way. "It's so good to see you again, I've missed you so much," she said giving me a huge hug. As usual there was an evening meal of flying fish followed by Nancy's famous bread and butter pudding. Later, we sat out on her veranda, enjoying the cool of the evening and trying to talk above the sound of the whistling frogs.

We met the contractor at the first of many trips across to St Margaret Church. We were not sure what to expect, but we were pleasantly surprised to see they had made real progress. Grace, who lives next to the church, called us over to tell us how happy she was to see the windmill wall being preserved and included as part of this project. Within a few minutes, Margaret Anne appeared and once again flung her arms around me. This lady has so much love to give and even though she had not seen Vanessa for many years, you would not have known. We felt like family coming home. Sheena found us at Margaret Anne's house, "I thought this would be where I would find you," she said getting out of the car. "I have just come from St Margaret's and seen the work. Very impressive."

We set off to meet the descendants Sheena knew and hadn't driven very far when we pulled up outside a house we had passed many times and often saw a gentleman sitting on the veranda. For this book I will call him Sonny. Sheena introduced us and then went inside to speak to the rest of the family. It was evident that he is quite a reserved man and having once been shy myself, I was careful not to embarrass him. After a while, he relaxed a little and told us how difficult it was to get work and how unfair the pay was. "They know I need to work and I don't complain about getting less than the others, but it's not right," he said. The injustice lives on. Nobody should be made to feel unworthy. I asked if he was okay with me explaining why we were there and I told him about the memorial and read the letter. Sheena reappeared. "What do you think about this?" she asked him. "Do you like the idea of the memorial?" "I think it's a good idea," he answered. As I handed him his invitation to the dedication that May, she added "Will you go Sonny?" "Yes, I will" came the reply. I could have hugged him. "Thank you," I said, "that will mean so much to us." What a change from the man we met initially. We even shared a joke or two before we left! Sheena enquired after his friend Jimmy (not his real name) and we heard that he had had a nasty accident and hurt his leg badly. He was still in great pain. "He's not here at the moment though," he said, much to Sheena's disappointment.

We headed off up the steep hill to Wilson's house. The last time I was with him, I had left my sunglasses behind, so I had told Margaret Anne to tell him not to worry but to give them to his daughter. However, when he saw me this time, his face lit up and he dashed off to retrieve them from the shelf. He was so happy to be able to give them back to me! When we stepped inside, we could hear Sheena chatting to someone in the back room. It turned out it was Jimmy. He was in a bad way. He told us about his accident, showing us his damaged leg. "I am in so much pain, I do not know what to do with myself," he said. Our hearts went out to him. He went on to say, "Do you know, I prayed this morning for God to send someone - and he sent you!" I caught Vanessa's eye and we smiled. Jimmy is about the same age as my eldest son and without being condescending, I desperately wanted him to know how much I cared. So, I tentatively asked if I could have a hug. "Sure," he replied happily. He seemed to calm down after this. After I told him and Wilson about the memorial, I asked if I could read the letter. Seeing the suffering here, a deep sadness welled up in me as I read and we could sense by their reaction, it had touched them too. We wanted to invite everyone personally, so each invitation had their name on it. "I'm really sorry Jimmy," I said, "but we left yours with your friend, Sonny." No sooner had I said it, than a face appeared through the window and there was Sonny, waving Jimmy's invitation. I do not know who was more surprised - him or us. Perfect timing! Sonny was no longer shy with us and he would wave enthusiastically whenever he saw us driving past. We had made a new friend and to be accepted in this community meant the world to us. We had time for just one more visit that day and went to see two brothers. They had already seen the memorial and described what we were doing as a 'fine gesture'. Sadly, some of the people Sheena was hoping to see had died since the last time she had been on the island. She was understandably upset. There was, however, one last couple she wanted to introduce us to, but they lived further away so that had to wait for another day.

Even though Sheena knew where this couple lived, it was not easy to find them again. So, after a few wrong turns, we were directed down a secluded track to a little house where we met Thomas and Mary. Thomas is quite a character and he had lots of stories to tell. However, Mary was quiet and explained she was not feeling too well that day, but was happy to sit and talk as this cheered her up. Not wanting to overwhelm them, I waited a while before telling them the story. Mary spoke very movingly about how this history still affected them. "Being ignored hurts," she said, "it's so unjust." Tears welled up so I passed her an Irish handkerchief I had been carrying around, waiting for the right person to give it to. "This represents all the tears that have been shed by you and your ancestors," I told her. "It was sent from a friend in Northern Ireland who asked me to give it to a lady who would understand." "I do," she said, "I do," Sheena asked what they thought of the memorial. "I think it's wonderful," Mary replied, "it will bring people together in love and unity." Knowing that this couple not only understood but could see the value of what we were doing, I asked if I could read the letter of apology. They smiled and nodded, and I couldn't help welling up with emotion as I read. Mary's response moved us deeply. Putting her hand on her chest, she said, "I receive that, heart to heart. I could tell how much you mean it." She even added, "Jesus was here." We could see she was getting tired, so decided it was time to leave. As we said our goodbyes, she gave me a huge hug. "I love you," she said, "I really love you." My word what an amazing visit this had been! As we walked out to the car, Thomas picked a flower from their bougainvillea bush and gave it to me with his love. A simple gesture that meant the world. I still have that precious gift, Thomas.

As we were in the area, we decided to visit Codrington College, the oldest Anglican Theological College in the Western Hemisphere, which we later discovered, has been affiliated with the University of Durham since 1875. Durham, of all places! We really could not make this up! The College sits high on a hill in St John, overlooking the Atlantic Ocean with the most spectacular views of the beautiful East Coast. We had been here several times before, but this time we hoped the principal might be able to spare us a few minutes to tell him about the memorial and its story. We explained to the lady in the office why we wanted to see him and she wanted to know more herself. She was desperately trying to take notes while I was speaking. "We have books and vision statements," Vanessa told her, "So don't worry about writing notes." She was relieved. She went on to ask if we believed this was our calling. "We certainly do," I replied, "we have been doing this for over 20 years." "Other people need to hear this," she said enthusiastically, reaching for the phone to book us an appointment with the principal. The College Registrar arrived and was equally interested in our story, "I have goose bumps," she said. "Our land desperately needs healing and this is what you are doing." She went on to ask, "Would it be possible for you to talk to the students about this?" My goodness. This had been a secret hope of mine, but I never imagined it would happen. "I would be happy to," I said, "even though it is totally outside my comfort zone." I could hardly believe what I had just agreed to! For someone who had a tough time at school to be speaking to students at a college - it confirmed to me the depth of the healing in my life.

The following day, the principal had been called to an urgent meeting, and we were ushered straight into a classroom of students from many different countries. Having never done anything like this before, I had no idea what to expect. When nobody introduced me, I knew I had just been thrown into the deep end. I quickly gathered my thoughts and explained to them that I was not a lecturer, but was going to tell them part of a long story, a story that spans many years and is connected to Barbados. It caught their attention. In closing, I told them, "This may not be your history, but each of us carry wounds from our past that can affect us personally. Ungodly actions against any group of people can lead to patterns repeating themselves. So, wherever you end up in your ministry, ask questions like; Where did this disunity come from? Did something happen that has never been dealt with? Are there people still carrying pain? Is there a root of anger? All injustice has consequences that could so easily affect you and your ministry. You do not need to go digging, but listen to people's stories and ask God for revelation as they share."

At the end, I asked if there were any questions. One young man raised his hand, "I don't have a question, but I have a comment to make," he said. "I am the only Bajan in this room. I have always known of the Poor White community, but I never knew their story. I had no idea how they came to the island. I want to thank you for revealing this to us." "Thank you," I replied, "hearing you say this makes everything worthwhile. I believe many people on the island who would say the same. These descendants deserve our respect and that is what my talk and this memorial are all about." The room was filled with fun and laughter afterwards as they all queued for copies of the vision statement and the letter. We gave them each a signed book and they wanted to have photos taken. I went there nervous, but I left elated. As we were making our way back to the car, we met the Executive Secretary of the trust. He told us he was extremely impressed with what we were doing and asked if next time I was on the island, could I return and share some more. Wow, I thought, laughing to myself, they may make a lecturer out of me yet!

Each one received a copy of "From History to Hope" from Shirley.

We had arranged to meet Sheena for the last time at Hunte's Gardens. It is a beautiful setting and a photographer's paradise, so Sheena was in her element. Despite everything we had done and the people we had met, Sheena expressed concern that she had not done enough. We reassured her, "What you have done has been amazing. You have opened doors we never could. We have waited so long for this; we cannot thank you enough." "Well, I wish I could have done more," she replied. She went on, "At the beginning, I was extremely anxious about how this would go. However, I have been immensely impressed with the way you have treated each person. What you are doing is giving them back their dignity." This was wonderful to hear from someone who has spent so many years fighting their cause.

We had met the most amazing people on this trip and tied up many loose ends. We felt ready to go home and look forward to the dedication ceremony in a few months.

Or so we thought……

CHAPTER 19

Stepping into Another World

Arriving home on that St Patrick's Day was strange, to say the least. It was as if we had entered another world, the world of coronavirus[16] (Covid-19), and we went straight into lockdown. Having not heard much of the news while we were away, we had little idea what was happening in the wider world and it was a shock! I was not allowed to leave the house, nor have anyone in, for the foreseeable future. I could not see my daughter and her family because of the vulnerability of her children; they had to be shielded to be kept safe. I wanted to hug my sons, but I was not allowed. I have never felt so alone, not even after Tony died, because then I had family around me. As travel ceased and airports shut down, it soon became apparent that we were not going to be able to return to Barbados in May.

As 2020 went on, the numbers infected with the Covid-19 virus began to drop and we started to think our return to Barbados later in the year might still be possible, although we couldn't make any firm commitment because of travel restrictions in place. I contacted church leaders on the island to see what they thought and received a reply from Canon Mayers. He proposed sometime around November 16, might be appropriate, as this is the Feast Day for the church's namesake, Saint Margaret of Scotland. As we pondered this thought, I researched this

---

[16] Coronavirus disease 2019 (COVID-19, also known as SARS-2) is a contagious disease caused by the coronavirus SARS-CoV-2 . In January 2020, the disease spread worldwide, resulting in the COVID-19 pandemic. Based on Johns Hopkins University statistics, the global death-to-case ratio is 1.02% (6,881,955/676,609,955) as of March 10, 2023.

lady. She was exiled during her youth and returned to England during the reign of her great-uncle, Edward the Confessor. I read about her life and discovered she was a godly woman. She worked hard to bring religious unity across Scotland and spent much of her energy caring for others, especially the poor and orphans. She tragically died at the age of 47, after hearing her husband and son had been killed in an ambush.

It was early September when we were finally able to meet in person to pray together. During this time, Vanessa felt it was important not to overlook St Margaret's Day, because Margaret was a significant lady. She also remembered the 'eureka' moment when we both realised St Margaret's church grounds was the perfect place to put the memorial. I decided to research more about the history of the church. It was built in 1862 by the Hon. J. A. Haynes, of Newcastle Plantation and named after his wife, Margaret Ann. The church was constructed on the site of the old Glenburnie Boiler House and much of the debris from the old boiler house was used in its construction. The original Glenburnie is in Fife, Scotland, so it has another connection to Scotland. It was all very confirming, but with the ongoing pandemic and travel restrictions, we all agreed that we should postpone the ceremony until 2021. Within a month of making this decision, the United Kingdom was put into a second lockdown, so the trip would have been impossible anyway. We had made the right choice.

Winter turned to Spring and it was a relief to see new shoots beginning to push their way through the soil as a real sign of hope. However, we heard the memorial garden in Barbados had not been so lucky. Covid restrictions and volcanic ash from an eruption on a nearby island had left the plants looking very sad. Our vision was always for a tranquil place where people could come and sit, enjoy the scenery, and remember those from generations past who suffered such injustice. We realised we needed to go back to help sort it out. To our delight, in July, the Barbados authorities announced that they were reopening their borders. We were so relieved, not just for us, but for the island itself as they rely so heavily on tourism. However, with strict restrictions still in place, it was clear that we would have to postpone the dedication ceremony for yet another year. Nevertheless, we believed we should still go to help with the garden and reconnect with as many friends and officials as we could while we were there.

So, once we had booked our flights, we were able to start making plans. We heard St Margaret's Church had a new minister, Reverend Anthony Harewood, and as we had no idea what he knew about the memorial, I arranged a meeting with him. We also discovered that a new Roman Catholic Bishop for Bridgetown, Neil Scantlebury, had been appointed. As so many of those transported were Catholics, we wanted to meet with him too. I also remembered Derek Fields, a singer/song writer from Barbados, who had contacted me after seeing the video about the project. He was interested in finding out more. So, I got in touch with him too. Everything for our next trip was in place.

CHAPTER 20

Island of Secrets and Surprises

Travelling during Covid meant a lot of regulations to follow and paperwork to organise, but with all our documents in place, we did not envisage any problems. Little did we know! The queues at Barbados airport were exceptionally long whilst they checked everyone's papers thoroughly before giving them a coloured wrist band. Most people were getting a green one, but for some random reason, we were given orange. I found myself being escorted by officials to a testing area, where I was required to have a further test. I then had to go into quarantine and was not allowed out of my hotel room until I received the test results. It was a lovely room with sea views and overlooking the pool, but I could not enjoy it. I woke desperate to know the result and get on with our itinerary. I took a quick look at my phone and was pleased to read 'Negative'. Great! However, I doubted myself after hearing my friend's result which read 'Covid undetected'. The different wording made me look up my result again. I had read it wrong! I had read the explanation of the result and it actually read, 'Covid detected'. I went into shock. I couldn't believe it. I had tested negative three days earlier and been extremely careful ever since. We had so many meetings booked and lots of work to do. What was going on?

I was reminded of someone we had met in Barbados with connections in government. I did not know if she could help, but contacted her anyway. She could not believe it either and said, "Send me copies of your documents from England and this result and I will see what I can do." The Hotel Manager rang to inform me that if a second test was positive, we would be moved to another hotel for 10 days isolation at our own expense. We were in sheer panic. Meanwhile, the original test was to be re-examined to see if there was another reason for the result. You can imagine my delight when our contact in the government called again. "Shirley," she said, "don't jump up and down or say anything to anyone until you hear officially, but when they looked at the system, your result was actually 'Covid not detected'. You are negative." She could not explain what had gone wrong and I did not really care! Minutes later, I received an official 'negative' certificate and an apology. It was a relief, but it had not been the start we hoped for!

At last, we were free to leave the hotel and so we made our way straight to St Margaret's and the Circle of Remembrance. It was my friend's first experience of driving in Barbados and they were shocked at the state of some roads. "These aren't potholes, they're craters!" They would say that more than once. This made me laugh, because they are far better than when we first came 13 years earlier! We arrived safely and were pleasantly surprised to see the garden in a better condition than we expected. Margaret Anne and Herbert had done an excellent job. Yes, it needed some work - the soil had dropped quite a bit and some plants had died - but with a bit of cutting back, the soil replenished and some new plants, it would look great again. With this settled in our minds, we decided to pay Margaret Anne a surprise visit. It was a surprise alright and when she saw us, she flung her arms in the air, letting out a squeal of delight, before giving us a tight hug.

We were saddened to hear that Hazel, Margaret Anne's sister, had been through a tough time and her health had suffered. We went to visit her and Margaret Anne had to call out several times before she appeared. The weight loss was obvious and she seemed reluctant to join us. I felt we needed to be careful. I tentatively said, "Surely you haven't forgotten me, Hazel."

There was no reply, so I continued, "Well, I haven't forgotten you and how you laughed at me when I fell off your wall." She chuckled. This was just what was needed to break the ice. It wasn't long before she began to share stories of how tough her childhood had been. "It is still like that now. No work, no money, no food," she said. Their main source of income was fishing, but this had become impossible, firstly because of Covid and then because of an unusual seaweed which trapped the flying fish. There were days when they had very little to eat. "But I still thank God," she said, "at least we do eat and we must be thankful." How challenging that was to us! "I don't go to church," she went on, "but I know God will look after us. I have faith for that." "This is church," I replied, "sharing our ups and downs, and how God has helped us through the hard times. This is church." We had been talking for some time when she suddenly asked if we could have a photo taken together. What a difference from when we first arrived. This was such a special moment!

The next day, we set off for Hunte's Gardens. We wanted to ask advice regarding the planting in the Circle of Remembrance. As the owner, Anthony Hunte, is a descendant, I also wondered if he would kindly donate a plant of his own. I was not expecting Anthony to remember me, but he did and before I even got a chance to say much, he was telling us that he had visited the memorial and was impressed. I knew this was the right time to ask for his help. "Shirley, I am only too happy to do something," he said and straight away, he was on the phone asking a local firm to donate compost, fertilizer, tools etc. The owner asked to speak to me and when I told him what the memorial was about, he was delighted to contribute. Furthermore, I did not need to ask Anthony to donate a plant, as he had already organised to give us 24! The next morning, our host, Ann Thomson, rang another firm in Bridgetown and again, after hearing what we were doing, they willingly gave all the soil we needed to refill the planters. We were promised everything we needed to start the work and it had not cost us a penny!

We had arranged to meet Derek, the singer-song writer, after church on Sunday. I could not help but wonder what he would be like. After the service, we drove Margaret Anne and Herbert home and Derek and his wife Lillian arrived soon after. We took an instant liking to this gentle giant with long hair who welcomed us with a big Bajan hug. We enjoyed listening as he and Margaret Anne reminisced and we discovered why the memorial meant so much to him. He is a Scottish descendant who cares deeply for the poor of Barbados. He wanted to uncover the truth about the so-called 'indentured servants' and whilst researching his family history, he discovered he had ancestors who had been married and buried at St Margaret's Church. His father owned a property close by too, so no wonder Martins Bay meant a lot to him. We wanted to hear more of his story, so when he offered to get lunch from his favourite restaurant on the island (which happens to be the only one in Martins Bay!), we were delighted. We took the food to his father's property and he told us the story of the house. Years earlier, Stephen, his father, had bought a piece of land with a small wooden dwelling on concrete pillars. Bit by bit, he built around this structure to create a beautiful, spacious house with a pool and stunning views over the magnificent east coast.

As we sat sharing stories, Derek and Lillian were astounded at how we had been led to Barbados. They felt the story of the indentured servants who came from the British Isles needed to be told. Derek said, "I can foresee people gathered around the memorial, to remember those who were transported centuries ago and to acknowledge that these people had also suffered." He continued, "It is no coincidence that you and Margaret Anne are now part of our lives. Some unseen hand seems to be behind this."

There were no celebrations planned on St Margaret's Feast Day because of Covid, but this left us free to work on the garden. That morning, Vanessa messaged and shared the scripture for the day in our Bible notes - Isaiah 55. It was perfect! It speaks of rain falling from Heaven and soaking the earth, causing it to sprout with new life, providing seed to sow and bread to eat. The trees flourishing where once there were thorn bushes, as a memorial to what the Lord has done. A few years ago, it was these verses that confirmed to us that the Circle of Remembrance was a God-given idea and it was a good day to be reminded of that.

Our first task that day was a meeting with Bishop Maxwell. To get to the Church Centre, we had to navigate a very tricky road. Try to imagine you are going down a steep hill, with another road, partly obscured and with no road markings, that cuts across in front of you and where few other drivers seemed to adhere to the rules of the road. We were both relieved to arrive safely! As we approached the bishop's office, we were aware of someone coming in behind us. It was St Margaret's new minister, Reverend Anthony Harewood. He informed us that he had been summoned by the bishop. I felt a moment of panic, but was immediately put at ease when the door opened and Bishop Maxwell welcomed us like old friends. We were joined by Archdeacon Eric Lynch too, who I had met previously. The unity in that room was tangible. I brought them up to date with all that had happened since we last met. I also shared the suggestion Derek and others had made to make the memorial a tourist destination. "But," I said, "for us, it is more about the truth being told and restoring dignity to those who have been affected over the years." They all agreed and suggested that the dedication ceremony be on St Margaret's Feast Day, November 16, the following year, 2022. They proposed it could be a time of celebration with food too. We were thrilled and made a promise to raise funds to help with costs. Before leaving, I shared my concern that due to the pandemic, we had not been able to re-visit all the descendants we had previously invited. Eric told us not to worry, for he had once been a Curate at St Margaret's, so he knew these people and guaranteed they would all get invitations.

This unity was also evident when we met the Catholic Bishop, Neil Scantlebury and he gave us a warm welcome. I started by asking him how much he knew about Arise Ministries. "I have looked at your website, watched the video and read your vision statement, and I'm about to start reading the book," he replied. We were impressed. However, he admitted he knew little of the Poor Whites and was shocked to hear the negative reactions some people had towards them. I shared as much as I could, including our visit in 2008. Knowing the Catholic people had suffered the most, I wanted to invite him to the dedication ceremony we had just arranged for the November. "I'll be there," he said immediately and even asked if there was anything they, the Catholic people, could do to help. This response touched us. Before we left, he prayed for us and the feeling of God's peace was so tangible that we were in tears. This was unity. No denominations. Just love.

Anthony had invited us back to Hunte's Gardens, so we tied it in with a meeting with Sally Miller, a publisher who Anthony introduced me to in 2019. However, the day did not start well. As we were crossing the road outside the apartment, I caught my foot on something which sent me sprawling and made my knee immediately swell up. One lady came to my aid and I am sure she had medical experience. She helped me back inside and told me to put ice on and rest it for the day. However, I knew I could not do that, this meeting with Sally was too important. So, we strapped ice to my knee and off we went. We spoke briefly to an English couple in the car park and then went up to the veranda where Sally was waiting. Sally had previously published articles about the Poor Whites in a magazine, the *Ins and Outs of Barbados*. Now she was considering covering the dedication ceremony and the history behind the memorial.

Afterwards, we joined Anthony and within a few minutes, the couple we had met outside arrived on the veranda. Anthony greeted them in his usual way, asking if this was their first visit, "No," the gentleman replied, "we have been coming here for over 20 years". With that Anthony invited them to sit, adding "Shirley here has an amazing story which I am sure you would love to hear." I was so embarrassed.

Chapter 20 - Island of Secrets and Surprises

"I'm so sorry," I said to them, "I know you didn't come here to listen to me, so I will share this as quickly as possible." When I had finished, the lady turned to me and said "I don't think you are going to like me very much." It was a surprising response, so I asked her why. "I am a direct descendant of Oliver Cromwell" she said. We could not believe our ears! We had a copy of *From History to Hope* with us and gave it to them. "I must tell you that this is written from a Christian perspective, for which I do not apologise," I said. The gentleman then introduced himself, "I'm David and this is my wife, Antonia. We want you to know that we are Christians too!" This was no chance meeting! I was in awe as we sat chatting with one of Cromwell's direct descendants. My word, this gets even more unbelievable! After a while, David asked if we would like some lunch. I told them that we had no plans and were happy to join them. They loved this side of the island and knew it well, so we followed them as they wound their way up a twisting narrow road that led to a restaurant up in the hills. I had no idea where we were until we walked inside. I could not believe what was in front of me - an unobstructed view of the Scottish district. It was truly breathtaking. It was a wonderful end to a perfect day.

With the joy of the day before still bubbling inside, we set off once more to join our friends at St Margaret's Church. I was looking forward to this and afterwards we planned to visit Fred Watson. I had met Fred a couple of times before, so I knew this would be another memorable moment. It had been nearly two years, so I was not expecting Fred to remember me. However, as I approached his tiny house, he was standing waving at me enthusiastically. "I thought you may have forgotten me," I said as I stepped inside. "Never," came the reply, "I never could forget you!" Fred shared a few stories, adding that he had been to see the memorial and found it very moving. I explained that sadly the dedication service had to be postponed until the following year. "Never mind, I still would like to be there," he added. "It will be a privilege to have you, Fred." I assured him. He bowed his head in acknowledgement of my words. What a gentleman!

Every individual has a story to tell and here in Barbados, they appreciate being given a voice. I have got to know Margaret Anne, Herbert and their family well. They all have their own stories to tell, but I never heard Margaret Anne ever feeling sorry for herself. In fact, it is exactly the opposite. She and Herbert have worked hard and are so thankful for everything they have and share their home with their extended family. They have embraced me as a member of their family and she now calls me her 'sister from another mother'. What an honour! Another thing that always impresses us is their generosity and this day was no different as we were invited to join them for lunch. I was glad we did, because as we were there, she received a call from Lillian inviting us all to her father-in-law's house close by. As Derek introduced us to Stephen, he said "These ladies, dad, are here telling the truth about how indentured servants came to the island." I do not think Stephen knew what to make of this information, but he welcomed us anyway. Recognising that not everyone understands our mission, we steered the conversation away. I had been told he was in a band called 'The Merrymen', so we talked about the band and their music. Stephen warmed to this and before long was sharing how they had travelled to many countries, including England, where they performed at places like the Royal Albert Hall and Trafalgar Square. This, I thought, was the story of a descendant who made good and had done some amazing things. However, he told us he had also suffered real pain. "I can talk about discrimination," he said, "because I have experienced it myself." It was heart-breaking to listen to his stories. Why should he suffer because of what Cromwell had done centuries ago to his ancestors? This was real, not something passed on like Chinese whispers. You could see the pain that was still there. I was concerned it had opened old wounds. I asked if I could read the letter of apology to him and Derek and he agreed. It had already been an emotional afternoon listening to their stories and the emotion spilled over as I read the letter. Margaret Anne and Derek put their hands on my shoulder and Derek graciously asked God to bless us and our town of Huntingdon. The tears flowed even more. As I presented them with a copy of the letter, I said to Stephen, "I believe God wants you to know that He never forgot you or your people. His love for you, and them, is, and has always been, unconditional." Stephen smiled "I know," he replied, "I can feel it. This has been a special day for me." I could not have been happier.

Stephen, Lillian and Derek receive the letter of apology from Shirley.

Throughout history, God has been blamed for wars and violence because of people like Cromwell, who believed He was on their side. So, we feel privileged to play a small part in bringing the truth to light. God is a God of love, not war. He never caused those people in the 17th Century to suffer - man did that.

That evening, we sat on the veranda, reminiscing and marvelling at the incredible events of the past few days. God had worked in ways so extraordinary that words almost failed us as we attempted to record it in the journal. As the sun dipped below the horizon, we watched in quiet awe, declaring it the perfect ending to a remarkable day."

CHAPTER 21

New Roots

Through that dark winter, it seemed forever waiting for signs of life in the garden. Eventually, though, spring arrived, and the buds on my magnolia tree started to burst into bloom. These flowers not only bring joy but are a reminder that life goes on. This gave me an idea. Over the years, we had lost some very dear friends from Ireland, England and Barbados. Perhaps we could honour them, and those deported, by planting a tree as a living tribute.

As I shared this thought with Annette and Vanessa, the idea grew. We decided to plant a tree in as many places as possible, as a symbol of healing, as it takes root in the land. Someone in Barbados had said, *"Cromwell's roots go so deep it will take some digging to get them out."* We know this to be true as we have been on this journey for many years and still meet people suffering from the consequences of his actions. The Bible symbolically speaks of the leaves of the trees that are for the healing of nations.[17] A nation in biblical times meant a people group. So, every tree we plant represents our love and respect for people, the opposite of how Cromwell had treated them. The first tree we planted was an olive in my garden in Huntingdon and the second, a magnolia, in Kelvin and Evaline's garden in Northern Ireland. We thought another could be in Barbados and offer shade beside the Circle of Remembrance.

---
[17] Ezekial 47:12b and Revelation 22:2.

We had plans to return to Barbados before the dedication to complete some remaining tasks, this would be the ideal time to plant this tree.

It was a beautiful June morning when we set off for the airport and this time our usual excitement was replaced with apprehension. The flight too turned out to be different from any we had done before. It began when a stewardess asked if we were going on holiday. "Not really," was my reply and I quickly explained about our work. She was intrigued. It was her first visit to Barbados and she knew nothing of the Poor Whites. So, I shared a small part of their history. As we sat ready for take-off, it became obvious she wanted to know more, so later I gave her a copy of *From History to Hope*. It made her day.

Later, another lady came over and started chatting. Her father was Bajan and she was returning to the island to honour him. We had plenty in common and, cutting a long story short, she was very interested in what we were doing. So, I gave her a book too. She returned later to say that she had already read to page 20 and was loving it, because it spoke into her situation. I then sat and listened for almost two hours as she poured out her life story. When she eventually returned to her seat, she said, "This has been the best trip ever!" All this and we had not even landed yet!

It was very hot and humid as we crossed the tarmac and into the airport terminal. I was relieved there was no hiccup getting through this time. Before setting off the next day, we had a time of quiet together. We began by listening to some worship songs Jonathan had recorded, and it was not long before we were all in tears. It was a precious moment. Our next task was to find new plants and a tree. The memorial garden is in full sun, so we needed plants that would stand these conditions. We began our search at a local nursery where the young lady advised us on what plants to buy, but they had no trees. We left there in search of a garden centre, and it was here we found a soursop tree. The assistant explained that it was high in vitamin C and known for its healing properties. She went on, "Many people make tea from the leaves as it is believed to help heart conditions, among other things."

Chapter 21 - New Roots

This was perfect!

The sun shone brightly the following morning as we set off for St Margaret's. It is so peaceful here. Margaret Anne and Herbert were already there and once again, we were welcomed with outstretched arms. Derek and Lillian arrived soon after. The ground was hard and it was hot work digging a hole for the tree and preparing the soil for the new plants we had bought. Once we had finished working, we stood deep in thought, when Derek walked over saying, "I have a song in my spirit" and he started to sing. The words of the chorus were perfect; *"Here I am Lord. It is I Lord, I have heard you calling in the night. I will go Lord, if you lead me, I will hold your people in my heart."* What a special moment! On the Sunday, we gathered again with friends to share a time of reflection. Derek brought his guitar and we finished by singing that same song once more. It was perfect! Annette, Vanessa and I returned a few days later to spend time privately. People who have visited the memorial garden have told us it is a special place. We agree. Heaven felt very close that day!

Next, we met up with Reverend Anthony Harewood at St John's Church to start planning the dedication ceremony. The church is a tourist destination and locals have stalls selling their crafts in the grounds. While looking around, we got chatting to one of the stall holders. He was very interested in the memorial, but I was shocked to hear he had never been down to St Margaret's because the roads were so bad. I gave him a copy of the book and hoped he would go to see the Circle of Remembrance for himself. We continued into the church and another gentleman, who we had seen there before, followed. He told us how touched he was by the way we spoke to his friend and wanted to come and chat to us himself. He started to ask a few questions and was impressed by how much I knew, especially regarding the poor. He started to tell us the history of the Red Legs/Poor Whites and how they came to Barbados, which, he said, was when they emptied the prisons in Ireland and Scotland. At that point, I had to correct him, and told him, "It's quite possible that some came from prisons, but the majority were Royalists and Catholics and came when Oliver Cromwell invaded their land and had them deported as prisoners of war." We stayed chatting for a while, sharing some of the story and he told us that I had given him a new perspective, for which he thanked God. We were thrilled and I am sure he will be passing this on to others too.

We revisited Fred, which we always loved to do, but this time, I had a special reason. As the oldest living descendant, I wanted to ask him if, at the dedication ceremony, he would be willing to accept the letter of apology on behalf of all the ancestors and people who had suffered down the centuries. He was moved by my request and bowed his head in respect before answering, "It will be an honour".

When we were last on the island, Margaret Anne had arranged to introduce us to her elderly aunt, affectionately known as Auntie Dorrie, who, in her nineties, was another of the older descendants on the island. We had been unable to go then, but being back in the bay, it felt like an ideal time and Hazel was willing to take us. We drove along an unmade road with stunning views of the coastline. Judy, Dorrie's daughter, came out to tell us that her mum was in bed and very poorly. This was a private time and we did not want to intrude, but after talking for a little while, she added that though her mum was too weak to talk, we could go in and see her. In the corner of the room was a picture of a handsome young man. "Who's this?" I asked, "That's my brother who tragically died over 10 years ago," Judy replied. She began to cry and I held her while she explained what had happened. I did not want to take advantage of her grief to tell her about our mission, but much later, the opportunity arose to share about the memorial. She was very interested, so I went on to explain about the letter of apology and, with her agreement, I read it. I was so moved by this family's story that I found it hard to contain my emotions. Judy took hold of me and Dorrie, raising her hand, tried her best to speak, but was far too weak. However, I believe she heard every word and felt the love that was in that room.

Before leaving Barbados, we made a visit to see our old friend, Jean, who hosted us for our first visit in 2008. She was also in bed, recovering from an operation, but pleased to see us. Amazingly, we discovered she lives next door to Derek's parents! We had met his mother, Diana, this trip too and she had told us her story. She is another firm believer that the truth of their ancestors needs to be told.

CHAPTER 22

Full Circle

Over the next few months, we were busy preparing for the dedication and feast. We were aware we couldn't go back in time to put things right, but we could show our respect to those who were treated so appallingly by sharing this feast with their descendants. This was to be a visible demonstration of how much they are loved and valued.

It had been 14 years since that first visit to Barbados in 2008 and it had often felt as though we were never going to reach this point, but finally we had. We have travelled thousands of miles over the years, meeting people from all walks of life. I had made eight trips to Barbados to realise this vision. It may sound glamorous, but it hasn't always been easy and it has been costly in so many ways. However, our love and commitment to the people and our passion to see the project through kept us going. So, we had mixed feelings as we landed in Barbados. It felt strange and there was some sadness, along with some excitement and even relief too.

We took the first opportunity to head off to Martins Bay to see our friends. Margaret Anne was going to introduce us to more descendants, but first I wanted to know how her Auntie Dorrie was doing. "She's still poorly," Margaret Anne informed me. "If you want to go down there, I would love to see her too," she said. As we entered their home, it was evident that things were not good. Dorrie was rambling as I sat holding her hand. "I don't know who I is," Dorrie said more than once. Her daughter repeatedly responded, "You're

Doreen King, mum." When she said it the next time, I answered for her and changed it to "You're Auntie Dorrie, that's who you is!"[18] Judy laughed, "You sound like a Bajan Shirley!" Sadly, Dorrie's condition deteriorated and the doctor, and then an ambulance came, so we left them alone. When I went back inside, Judy was holding her mother's hand and the sadness on her face made it very clear how hard this was for her. "We didn't want her to go to hospital," she said. "Please will you pray for us Shirley?" It was a real privilege! I took Dorrie's hands and looked into her eyes. I spoke the words Jesus spoke to his disciples before his death,[19] but inserted her name, "Dorrie, Jesus says, my peace I leave with you, my peace I give to you, not like this world gives, give I to you, Dorrie. Let not your heart be troubled and don't be afraid." Dorrie died peacefully in her daughter's arms the following day. What a tender and loving way to leave this world!

Our first scheduled meeting was with the Catholic Bishop Neil Scantlebury. It was good to see him again. He welcomed us warmly, and I shared the arrangements for the dedication with him. He was delighted to receive his invitation. However, I needed to ask him an awkward question. When I was last with him, I had presented him with the original framed letter of apology, but as I planned to present copies again at the ceremony, I needed to ask for it back. Before I could ask the question, he laughed saying, "Are you telling me you want it back?" We all laughed as I replied, "Yes, please!" I explained that he would get it back, along with another letter written especially for the Catholic Church, which I had originally presented to Father Harcourt at the Reconciliation Service in St Patrick's Cathedral in 2008. You could see the surprise on his face. "Father Harcourt," he exclaimed. "He is here on the island and I will be seeing him this afternoon." We could hardly believe our ears! Harcourt has been such an important part of our Barbados story, but as he spends so much time overseas, it had been hard to keep in touch with him. We were delighted he was on the island and left an invitation for him too. It

---

[18] Spoken in local/dialectal style to reflect natural speech.
[19] John 14:27.

felt like things were coming full circle.

We left feeling very encouraged and set off north to St Nicholas Abbey. We had an appointment with Larry Warren, the owner, who Father Harcourt had introduced us to back in 2008. As this old plantation house is a significant part of the island's history, I wanted to share the background to the memorial and give him a personal invitation. "I remember you, Shirley," Larry said from across the room. I was astonished. He told me that they have a great interest in the plight of the Irish during the Cromwellian period. Even though his family arrived on the island much later, he thought it possible though that they had descendants in their family tree and so was happy to accept our invitation. He invited us to stay and have lunch. We felt honoured and accepted gladly. What a treat that was!

As we left St Nicholas Abbey, we thought it would be an opportunity to revisit the cave in Speightstown where, during the 17th Century, the Catholic people secretly celebrated Mass. We knew we were close by, but had no idea exactly where it was. We pulled into a petrol station and Annette boldly asked a gentleman in the car beside us if he could help. He apologised, saying he had no idea where it might be, but he knew a man who might. After a quick phone call, he told us to follow him. His friend was busy mending his roof when he got the call, but immediately stopped work to take us up the hill to a cave he thought we might mean. Sadly, it was not the right one. Disappointed, they asked what this was all about. They were amazed and told us, "Most people come to Barbados on holiday, but you don't, you genuinely care for our land and its people." His face lit up as he had another idea of another cave which, thankfully, was the right one. Before leaving us, he concluded, "This is a spiritual thing you are doing."

Vanessa and Annette praying in the cave.

We also had a meeting with Hon. Charles Griffith, the Member of Parliament for St John, who Annette and I met in 2019. I shared with him the progress over the years and he was astonished to hear some of the stories. He certainly encouraged us and commented on how pleased he was that the memorial was in his constituency. Another person who greatly encouraged us was Peter, the head of the company hired to do the catering for the feast. He wanted to know more about the project and was blown away by the story I shared. He described it as a 'game changer' and believed it would bring people on the island together. "Big things will come of this, you'll see," he concluded.

With all our appointments over, it was time for us to move to Martins Bay. We wanted to stay on this side of the island so we could mingle with the locals and hopefully catch up with a few of the people we had met before, including Jimmy. Vanessa and I met him in 2020 when he was in a bad way after a nasty accident. We were disappointed to learn he was not around much anymore. As we last saw Jimmy at the home of our friend Wilson, we decided to go and visit his daughter. Wilson sadly had since passed away. As we left her home, we spotted a familiar figure in the distance, walking towards us in Wellington boots. It was Jimmy! We were delighted and thrilled to see he was walking a little better too. His face was a picture and it was obvious he was as happy to see us as we were to see him. I turned and looked over at Wilson's daughter, who had a big smile on her face. The love her father had for this man was still there. I shared the news about the dedication service and the meal afterwards, adding, "We would love to see you there, Jimmy." With a huge smile, he replied, "I will be there. I promise I will come," he said more than once. He had made our day!

It was extremely humid that evening, so we decided to have our supper outside under the stars. We chatted about the day, remarking how God had been in every moment, before sitting back and taking in the most amazing sight above us. No light pollution here, we could see thousands and thousands of stars and the occasional shooting star too. We have never seen the night sky so clear! We had sat there for maybe an hour or two when we spotted a bright red light on the horizon. We weren't sure what it was. As we watched, it grew larger and larger, and we could see it was a red moon, rising. It was such an awesome sight! Never having seen a red moon quite like it before, we read up about it and learned it is associated with harvest and a sign of change. Early the following day, when Vanessa was enjoying a morning swim, she spotted a rainbow over the church. First the red moon, now a rainbow. We took it as a real sign of hope and the promise of restoration.

Early one morning, I received a phone call from a Barbadian businessman, John, who was at the memorial and wanted to find out more information. As we were staying only a stone's throw away, I invited him to come round. I wondered how he found out about us and soon discovered it was through his sister-in-law Jan, who we met in the pool where we stayed the previous week. When we met her, she was reading a book on white slavery and was intrigued by what we were doing. As John is a descendant of an indentured servant from Scotland, he was interested in the story of the memorial and wanted to share his own story too. I began by telling him a small part of our journey, just enough to help him understand why we were doing this. It was evident he was impressed and totally understood the need to say sorry. His ancestors had been promised land after years of hard labour, but being illiterate, they were no sooner given it, than it was taken off them. The paper they had signed with an 'X' was worthless. "Many claim these people weren't slaves, but if anyone worked without pay, they were slaves," he said emphatically, as he showed us his documents as proof, if ever we needed it. "I am not seeking financial reparation," he added, "what I want is Scottish citizenship - the acknowledgement and recognition that Scotland is my ancestral homeland." He left promising to come to the dedication ceremony. We felt so fortunate to have met John and spend this time with him.

We planned to have a little down time, so we headed off to Hunte's Gardens to enjoy the peace and tranquillity of this bit of paradise for a final time this visit. Anthony spotted me as we entered the veranda. As usual, he teased me a bit before introducing me to his guests, around 15 of them. I had no idea he was going to do this, but once again, he handed over to me to tell my story. After a while, Anthony spoke up, "Do you know how I know this is authentic? Because it never changes. It is always the same."

Staying in the area made it easy to attend St Margaret's Feast Day service. The church was packed and among the congregation was Reverend Father Taitt, the minister who was leading the service when I first shared the vision for the memorial back in 2019. We had not seen him since, so it was wonderful to reconnect with him. He greeted me like an old friend, saying how thrilled he was to see the memorial complete and what an incredible sight it was. I asked him if he was planning to come on Saturday and he almost fell backwards, answering enthusiastically, "Of course I am. I would not miss this wonderful occasion for anything."

Another significant encounter in 2019 was with Grace and Jacques, who live next to St Margaret's Church. As the memorial would be adjacent to their property, we felt it was important to share the proposed plans. Grace was delighted to hear that the remains of the windmill would be incorporated. "It's our heritage and part of our story," she said, "That's why it means so much to me." Sadly, when we visited her this time, Grace wasn't too well and was finding it very difficult to walk. "Even so," she said resolutely, "I will do my very best to be at the dedication."

We have met many descendants over the years, both Black and White, rich and poor. All, like Grace, were delighted that their story is now being told and their ancestors were, at last, being recognised as part of Barbados history.

CHAPTER 23

Celebrations of Remembrance

The long-awaited day finally arrived. We had offered to help with preparations, so early that morning we made our way to St Margaret's Church. As we turned the corner, we were met with the beautiful sight of white gazebos with tables and chairs already set up for 100 people. It looked just like a wedding!

We were excited and a little apprehensive. We had done all we could, but would the people come? To our delight, we watched as people made their way down the hill. Some of the first to arrive were Stephen and Diana, Derek's parents. Stephen greeted me with a warm hug. I was so pleased to see him. Annette accompanied Diana to see the memorial stone and she described how happy she was, "It's wonderful," she said, "and these wildflowers growing in the windmill wall are used for healing."

John kept his promise and arrived shortly after, accompanied by his wife and her sister, Jan. Later, with tears in her eyes and her hand resting over her heart, Jan came to me and said, 'My healing has begun.'

To my joy, I caught sight of an elegant figure walking very slowly towards us. It was Grace! "It's a long time since I was this happy," she said as I joined her. "I have waited so long for this to happen and this story to be told." At the end of the ceremony, I went over to ask what she thought. She lifted her hands to Heaven, smiled her beautiful smile, closed her eyes and took a deep sigh of contentment. No words were necessary.

Memorial garden in bloom for our guests.

As people kept arriving, I kept an eye open for Fred as he had a key role to play in this ceremony. We had offered to pick him up, but being independent, he said he would be fine. To our surprise, a bus pulled up and Fred got off, looking so smart with his Queen's Medal pinned to his jacket. I felt proud and also relieved to see him. The people kept coming and I spotted Father Harcourt. "I can't believe this Shirley," he said as I joined him, "I was only on the island to get my eyes done and here I am sharing this wonderful day and this remarkable thing you have done here." During my talk later, I wanted to honour him. "If it was not for this man," I said, "we might not be here today. He was the first descendent to invite us to Barbados in 2008." I turned towards him and he took my hand in such a way that said, 'This bond can never be broken.'

Reverend Harewood had done a wonderful job planning the ceremony. As Canon Mayers was unable to attend, the words he had prepared in 2020 were read on his behalf;

> *"It was sometime towards the end of the first quarter of 2019 that I received a small delegation, led by Mrs Shirley Bowers, in my office at St John's Parish Church. She proceeded to explain why they were in Barbados and to share the conviction they had for the project we bless today. They were not the first I had heard from. This group seemed more passionate and they were determined not to be mere seekers, but finishers. They had a clear philosophical under-pinning of their belief and conviction that their proposed actions were the correct ones. They raised that interesting question in my mind, 'Can one generation apologise for the sins of a previous generation?' I felt their project was one I was willing to invest some time and energy. Once I had committed myself, we started looking for a way forward. The exact location is the site of a former windmill. We felt the remnants of this mill would tie the history of sugar and the presence of these indentured servants and forgotten people together in a circle of remembrance.*
>
> *Today as we remember, we gather again to recognise the past and try to envision a new future."*

It was my turn to speak next. How things have changed! Years ago, I would have been horrified to stand up in front of people, let alone a monsignor, two bishops, an archdeacon, and three priests. I would have thought like Moses; 'Who am I to speak?' and 'What can I say?' However, it is different now. I simply do what I feel called to do—to tell this story and the miraculous signs that have led us along the way. Regardless of whether the listener is a Poor White or a bishop, it makes no difference. The most important thing is to tell the truth. Everyone listened intently as I shared; "When I became aware of

Cromwell's action all those years ago, God put an ache in me that is hard to explain. It was an ache I couldn't ignore. Hence, I have spent over 25 years seeking to bring healing and reconciliation to this part of history. Discovering how your ancestors had been treated by Cromwell, in the name of God, this broke our hearts. We believe beyond doubt that this was man's inhumanity to man and not God's plan." I went on to read the verses in Romans 9, telling them we believed this was what God would say to them now;

> *"To those who were rejected and not my people, I will say to them 'You are mine'. And to those who were unloved I will say, 'You are loved. And in the place where they were told 'You are nobody,' this will be the very place where they will be renamed 'Children of the living God'.*

As I read these powerful words from the Passion Translation, you could feel the love around.

It was then time to read and present the letters of apology, starting with the descendants. As I escorted Fred to the front, I told everyone, "Fred is 96 and the oldest direct descendant on the island. He has kindly agreed to represent all the ancestors and their descendants who we are honouring today." I heard a gasp at his age, then came the applause for him. This was such a privilege! Once again, I felt extremely emotional as I started to read. Fred responded with a big smile and a heartfelt 'thank you'. He sadly passed away in 2024, before we had the opportunity to visit him again, but I know he felt as honoured as we did that day and this letter would have taken pride of place on his wall. Bishop Maxwell received the letter on behalf of St Margaret's Church and as the Member of Parliament had been unable to come, our friend Jessica who works for the government, received it on his behalf. I then invited Bishop Scantlebury to join me while I explained that I was presenting him with a different letter, one that had been written especially for the Catholic people in 2008. I had barely started to read when I spotted the tall, unmistakable figure of Jimmy walking down the hill, still wearing his wellington boots, coming towards us and waving at me. It was very important to acknowledge his arrival so, after apologising to Bishop Neil for the interruption, I asked everyone to give him a warm welcome. They all applauded and he responded by putting both hands on his heart. He later came over to tell me how sorry he was to be late. That didn't matter, I told him, what mattered was that he came. "I wanted to be here," he said. "I love you guys and I wasn't going to let you down." That for me was the cherry on the cake. Many people told us afterwards how touched they were by the love and respect we showed for both Fred and Jimmy.

The ceremony continued as Derek sang a song, *'Hearts and Souls and Spirits'* that he had written especially for this occasion. What made this so special was it came from the heart of a descendant. Part of it is reproduced below;

Hearts and Souls and Spirits

A song it is rising in my heart
The tribes of our people forgotten, torn apart
Circles of memories from ripples of pain
Cast from your shores, can you hear your name?

From the lands of green and the mountains high
We were cast on the shores
of the Islands of blue sky
No longer forgotten, we're free men for sure
In the Circle of Memories
Where the wild seas roar

*Come na Redlegs, wherever you are
We're one family, alive in God's Heart
Bone of my bone, and flesh of my flesh
My brother, my sister, my kin, thou art.*

The Venerable Eric Lynch, Archdeacon of Barbados and a former Curate of St Margaret's Church, spoke of his memories before he dedicated the Circle of Remembrance. He blessed it to be;

> *"A quiet place for those who need rest. A joyful place, delighting the senses. A peaceful place, reviving the servant-hearted. May the flowers remind us to keep blooming. May the benches remind us to stop and rest. May the tree remind us to root ourselves in Christ and shelter one another in grace. In every season may this garden welcome our neighbours."*

Finally, Bishop Maxwell (Anglican) and Bishop Scantlebury (Catholic) walked over to the memorial and Reverend Small-Warner, the Assistant Curate, and I followed. It was the climax of the afternoon as both bishops unveiled the memorial stone together. Total unity!

The memorial stone was officially unveiled.

Bishop Maxwell read the words aloud for all to hear;

Following the conquest of Ireland by Oliver Cromwell in 1649, Prisoners of War, Royalists, Catholics, and many others were taken from their lands of Ireland, Scotland, England, and Wales and transported to Barbados against their will.

This memorial is in honour of them and their descendants because every life matters.

"*Those who sow in tears will reap with songs of joy*" Psalm 126

Memorial erected in 2020 by Arise Ministries from Huntingdon, England, the birthplace of Oliver Cromwell.

The Memorial Stone

With the official ceremony over, it was time for the feast. The atmosphere was buzzing as the poorest of the Poor White descendants shared a meal alongside the richest. The food was delicious and we watched contentedly as old friendships were renewed and new ones made. Mingling with the guests, both Black and White, was a joy for us. Many expressed how moved they had been and how important it was for this story to be told. One such conversation was with Simon, Larry Warren's son. Whilst I was speaking, I was aware how intently he was listening. We had a framed copy of the letter which I felt was for St Nicholas Abbey and when I gave it to him, he was thrilled. He told me that the letter will become part of their story at the abbey and they will encourage people to come and visit the memorial for themselves. What more could we ask! I was delighted later to hear from Larry, "Simon mentioned he was really moved by what you have done and like him, many in Barbados will appreciate the recognition you have given to those who perished and lived enslaved, including the effect on their many descendants. This dedication can also bring a focus on our history for future generations to reflect on and to further investigate for themselves in order that it is not forgotten."

After the feast, we went inside the church to watch the Barbados Memorial Project video that Jonathan had produced. This also gave me the opportunity to share more of the miraculous ways in which we had been led. I began by sharing the 'I am who I am because of everyone' story from the airport (Chapter 5). I could see the astonishment on their faces as the photograph of it came up on the screen. "From that moment on," I told them, "we have never doubted that this was part of God's plan and it has been confirmed many times." As an example, I told them how we had met Antonia and David at Hunte's Gardens the year before. "Antonia is a direct descendant of Oliver Cromwell," I explained, as her photo came up on the screen. "Here she is at the memorial with her son, only a few weeks ago." Well, that blew their minds! One young man who had looked as if he was not particularly listening, lifted his head and I could see him mouth 'Wow, wow, wow'.

Antonia and her son James, direct descendants of Oliver Cromwell visit the memorial.

As the day came to an end, we were overwhelmed by how many people wanted to speak to us, wanting to show their appreciation. One lady came rushing to me, asking for a big hug. Last, but not least, our dear friend Reverend Father Taitt was clearly very emotional and moved by it all. He told me, "It's been a wonderful day and a real privilege for me to have been here at the beginning and now at the end." As we were gathering our things together, Father Harcourt introduced me to one of his former students, Reverend Nicholas Small-Warner, who was the Assistant Curate at St Margaret's Church. Nicholas asked if we had ever been to Codrington Theological College. It suddenly hit me, to my astonishment, we had met before. Back in 2020, when I had spoken to a group of students at the college, at the end of my talk, he was the student who thanked me for telling this story. He said he was the only Bajan in the room and he had always known of the

Poor White community, but never knew their story, or how they came to the island. We have told this story many times since, as it helps people appreciate just how misunderstood the Poor White descendants are. Fast forward two and a half years and that same young student is now Assistant Curate at St Margaret's and took an active role in the service. Once again, you really couldn't make this up! The following morning, he was taking the service and asked if I would say a few words. Of course, it was his story I had to tell! He stood beside me as I spoke and I could feel his joy. The congregation too responded with spontaneous applause.

It was hard to leave the friends we have made over the years. One church member said as we left, "Shirley you have been here so many times you are one of us now!" What an honour. Margaret Anne and Hazel were in tears, they did not want us to go. We really are family.

**Tears followed by joy as Shirley promises
Margaret Anne that they would be back.**

Before heading to the airport, we kept our promise to visit Stephen. He told us how moved he was by all we had accomplished and the spirit in which it had been done. It was good to hear this from someone who is a direct descendant. To our surprise, he called himself a 'Red Leg' and spoke more of how much he had suffered in the past because of that. It was sad to hear these stories, but very important for him to tell them. It is part of his healing. I reached out and, touching his arm, said, "No matter what Stephen, God loves everyone equally. And that includes you!"

Our work on the island was done!

**

As this story draws to a close, I return to that young man whose face I saw at the beginning and his words, "Thank you for telling my story". I asked the question, how are we connected? I hope this book answers that. It is God's love; His love for that young man and all those who suffered, as well as their descendants; His love that saw the injustice and pain; His love that longs to restore and bring healing; His love that inspired us and filled us with the same longing for restoration and healing; His love for each of us. That is what connects us.

One thing I can say for sure is that young man's face was always with us. No matter where we went, he was there. We are kin and kinship, I heard someone say, is born from love and out of that love, comes justice. So many people in Barbados have become our kin. So young man, it has been a privilege to travel this journey with you. I pray we have done you, and the thousands you represent, justice. We may not know your names, but you will never be forgotten again, because each one of you matters.

Rest in peace, my friend. I heard your cry. Your story has been told.

CONTACT DETAILS

To contact Shirley or Arise Team

Visit

www.AriseMinistries.co.uk

INSPIRED TO WRITE A BOOK?

Contact

Maurice Wylie Media

Your Inspirational & Christian Book Publisher

Specialist in Life Stories

Based in Northern Ireland and distributing around the world.
www.MauriceWylieMedia.com